MUSEUMS OF
CRACOW

Collegium Maius, oldest building of Jagellonian University in Cracow, now the University Museum.

MUSEUMS OF
CRACOW

Newsweek / GREAT MUSEUMS OF THE WORLD

NEW YORK, N.Y.

**GREAT MUSEUMS
OF THE WORLD**

Polish Editor: Izabela Kunińska

American Editor: Henry A. La Farge

MUSEUMS OF
CRACOW

Introduction by:
Tadeusz Chruścicki

Commentary texts by:
Franciszek Stolot

Translation by:
Edward Rothert

Art Editors:
Virilij Dariš
Izabela Kunińska

Published by:
NEWSWEEK, INC.
& ARNOLDO MONDADORI EDITORE

ISBN 0-88225-245-3

Library of Congress 82-48023

INTRODUCTION

Tadeusz Chruscicki, *Director*
National Museum of Cracow

This book is devoted to the art collections of Cracow museums and other institutions which are museums in all but name inasmuch as their treasures are also on public display. All share the unique physical setting of a city steeped in historical and artistic atmosphere. As Cracow itself constitutes a museum, it has seemed necessary to cull the material from various collections rather than from a single museum. Much of the material survives outside the walls of museums proper, remaining in the setting to which it originally belonged, a condition that is obvious on the spot but hard to capture on the printed page. This is the case with works of art in architectural monuments such as the Royal Castle and the Cathedral on Wawel Hill, numerous other churches and palaces, famous public buildings, and old burghers' mansions. These works have preserved their esthetic qualities in the places for which they were originally intended and merge with what has been assigned by history to the safekeeping of museums, gratifying the age-old need to commune in our daily lives with values of a higher order and feel the continuity of human culture and its achievements.

Poland's emergence as a state toward the end of the 10th century coincided with the culmination of the Romanesque period whose art styles she proceeded to assimilate. As a result, lasting links were forged with Latin culture, at first mostly through the intermediary of Moravia and then Bohemia to the south. In due course the relations with Rome and the Empire became more direct, and the universal patterns of European cultural experience stemming from its chief sources took root and stamped themselves on the centuries that followed.

Art historians use the term "artistic capital" for places which at different times have grown into firmly established centers in the diffusion of universal ideas and currents in art, and as the dominant influence in the culture of areas which have acquired an autonomous identity by a combination of various political, economic, ethnic and other factors.

Cracow unquestionably belongs in this category not only because of the role it has played in the cultural history, past and present, of Poland, but also of the place it occupies in the European heritage. For some five hundred years, from the early Middle Ages to the close of the 16th century, Cracow was also the political capital of Poland. Much later it was spared the devastation suffered elsewhere in the last and most brutal of world wars. Today it is enjoying a third "golden age" and belongs among the monuments of the world's cultural heritage placed under special care and protection.

The first heyday in the city's fortunes stretched from the Middle Ages to the Renaissance, when it basked in the brilliance shed by the glittering and stimulating life of the royal court of Wawel Hill. As the kingdom of the last rulers of the Piast line and the succeeding Jagiello dynasty grew in power and wealth and climbed to an important political and economic position in Europe, Cracow became the hub of intercourse with the whole cultural world of the time and was itself a hive of ideas, influences and creativity which fanned out over the vast territory of Poland and beyond.

The works of architecture, which already at that early date demarcated the city's functional structure, centered around the largest market square in contemporary Europe and a magnificent Cloth Hall which has survived to the present day, adjacent to Wawel Hill on which stand the old royal castle and the cathedral complex. Complementing these was an increasingly rich repertoire of painting and sculpture, goldsmith's work, embroidery and other crafts. These splendors were matched by a flowering of poetry, philosophy and many sciences (especially during the Renaissance), and even art collecting.

The transfer of the principal royal residence from Cracow to Warsaw at the beginning of the 17th century marked not only the end of the city's metropolitan role, but also coincided with the onset of a political and economic decline in the life of Polish towns in general. In this check to urban intellectual and artistic development, Cracow was also a victim. Although building still flourished, producing some fine Baroque churches and imposing noblemen's houses, it was too desultory to alter the general trend.

The fall of Poland, sealed in 1795 by the partitioning of the whole of her territory between the neighboring powers of Austria, Prussia and Russia, ushered in more than a century of national bondage, bleak years of despair relieved only by the flashes of hope kindled by insurrections, but ruthlessly extinguished by the overwhelming might of the occupiers.

The natural longing of the whole Polish people for restoration of a free and independent state was expressed not solely through uprisings (which, for that matter, produced no effective results). It also took the form of a tenacious day-to-day cultivation, elevated spontaneously into a patriotic duty, of the Polish ethos and of all kinds of scholarly, cultural and artistic endeavors fueled by national traditions. Various associations and institutions were formed for this purpose and acted as the political surrogate of a disenfranchised society. Cracow, the former capital in happier days, its antiquities a symbol of Poland's past glory and might, again became the focus of Polish aspirations and a rallying point for all three partition zones. Thus when the Austrian regime in southern Poland was liberalized in 1867 and the city acquired a limited degree of autonomy, there followed a remarkable upsurge of Polish intellectual and artistic life and the institutions organizing it.

Having in this way been called upon to act as the spiritual capital of the Polish people, Cracow entered its second "golden age." At Jagiellonian University Polish was restored as the language of instruction and outstanding scholars from all parts of the country joined the faculty. In 1873 the Cracow Learned Society was transformed into a national Academy of Learning. The humanities in particular thrived, and the first departments of archaeology and art history came into being.

To the School of Fine Arts, of which Jan Matejko became principal in 1873, flocked the pick of the nation's painters and sculptors, while Matejko's own work was a source of general inspiration. In 1854 a Society of Friends of the Fine Arts had been formed and began to hold exhibitions and purchase paintings with the idea of eventually organizing a national museum. In 1876 the Czartoryski Collection was brought back from Paris and three years later, with the help of contributions and gifts from the public, Poland's first National Museum was opened in Cracow, its chief aim being the patriotic one of a propagation of national history and art. It was to be the model for the vast majority of museums of all sizes subsequently established in Poland.

Art in Poland had always evolved in close relationship with trends in Europe. Works representing its different schools had been imported in quantity, as inventories of the collections assembled in the 16th, 17th and 18th centuries testify. Museums were unable, however, to do justice to this abundance as by the time that acquisitions were being made in the latter half of the 19th century the general impoverishment of the country, the losses suffered in wars and the punitive confiscations that followed each of the risings had taken a heavy toll of Polish-owned works of Euoprean art. Those that found their way into the museums are only a vestige of the riches of the past. Even so, they still repay interest as among them are paintings by Leonardo and Rembrandt, and they have accordingly been included in the final section of this publication.

Until the beginning of the 20th century Cracow remained the fountainhead of the most buoyant and noteworthy currents in Polish art. It was the base of a great many history and genre painters in the Matejko manner and the scene of the Modernist explosion of Young Poland sparked by the remarkable talents of Stanislaw Wyspianski and Jozef Mehoffer. It is in Cracow too, in its National Museum, that their work can be admired in its greatest variety.

Cracow is still Poland's most beautiful city and, second to Warsaw, its biggest center of learning and art. With its museums and antiquities now paralleled by contemporary achievement, it arouses general interest among foreign as well as Polish visitors.

Surveying its seven-century history of art, we see a great variety of schools and styles, and a host of artists of arresting individuality and powers of expression. It is for the reader to judge the extent to which, while embracing the universal ideals of their times, they succeeded in stamping their works with the *genius loci* and giving them a distinct shape through the vibrancy of their imagination and the beauty and purity of their technical accomplishment.

The earliest records of an interest in collecting precious and artistic objects in Cracow go back to the Middle Ages. It is from these times—the 12th century—that we have the first lists of the contents of the Treasure-house of Wawel Cathedral—a very special church as it is the one in which almost all the kings of Poland were crowned and eventually laid to rest.

Despite the ravages of war and years of bondage, its collection of liturgical objects and vestments, insignia, paintings, sculptures, furniture, tapestries and the like is one of the most valuable in Poland and has long been open to the public in an extension to the Cathedral added in the 15th century. Together with superb examples of illumination in the adjoining Chapterhouse Library and the magnificent works of art adorning the interior of the Cathedral itself—which, apart from performing its religious functions, has for centuries been an object of esthetic wonder and contemplation—all these things add up to a dazzling living organism which at the same time meets the standard requirements for their preservation.

The oldest collections of a strictly museum type belong to Jagiellonian University founded in 1364. These began to be formed in 1400, when the university was reinstated and reorganized, with gifts and bequests from its eminent patrons, teachers and alumni. Together with the university library assembled in a similar way, all these treasures were placed in a wing—specially built for the purpose in 1515–19—of Collegium Maius, an edifice which has survived to the present day and is rated among the finest monuments of Gothic architecture in the city. This building, now the seat of the Jagiellonian University Museum, houses not only antiquities and works of art, but also a splendid collection of scientific instruments lovingly preserved ever since they were first acquired. On the other hand, the Jagiellonian Library—with its huge stock of illuminated manuscripts, old books, maps and prints—was moved in our century to a modern building in a new section of the city.

In the first half of the 15th century, almost concurrently with the University collections, there came into being in the cloisters of a nearby Franciscan monastery a painting gallery of a singular kind which still draws many sightseers. It comprises portraits of bishops of Cracow, the earliest being mural paintings executed immediately after the erection of that Gothic edifice in 1436–55. This gallery, systematically enriched with more murals—some on allegorical themes—and also with easel portraits, has continued to be enlarged in contemporary times, providing a striking display of paintings in various modes which, apart from their historical interest, constitute a museum of considerable artistic value, making it possible to follow the evolution of Cracow painting from one age to another. Together with the paintings and stained-glass in the abbey church—among which the late 19th-century works of Stanislaw Wyspianski are in themselves masterpieces of Polish art—these form yet another aspect of Cracow's heritage in which museum functions blend with a living historical and artistic fabric.

The supreme example of such fusion is the castle on Wawel Hill which during the reigns of the Piast and Jagiello kings was the seat of the court and now houses one of the most magnificent and famous museums in Poland. In its present form it is a Renaissance *palazzo* enclosing an arcaded quadrangle, the outcome of the conversions undertaken by King Sigismund I (1506–48) at the beginning of the 16th century. Within its walls are preserved the remnants of Romanesque buildings and the Gothic castle that had previously stood on this site. The architecture of the palace provides a natural and stately setting for its accumulations of art, among which pride of place belongs, next to the objects in the old Treasure-house and Armory, the famous set of tapestries commissioned by Sigismund II (1548–72) in Brussels in the 16th century to decorate the interiors of his residence. In the history of Polish art these occupy a special place for the additional reason that in 1571 Sigismund II—the last of the Jagiello line—bequeathed them to the nation, so that we can date the origins of art collecting at Wawel as far back in history as the 16th century.

The Treasure-house along with the monumental architecture and interior of the Gothic Church of Our Lady which stands in Market Square offer yet another wonderful example of the way in which the typical functions of a museum are harmoniously dovetailed with a historic building which for centuries has served its original purpose unchanged.

The Treasure-house is a quadrangular, Mannerist addition built around 1600, containing amidst the Baroque *décor* of interiors specially adapted for the purpose a rich collection of goldsmith's work, vestments and other liturgical objects. These are nevertheless somewhat overshadowed by the propinquity of the high altar of the church itself, comprising the soaring polyptych carved toward the end of the 15th century by Veit Stoss with a sweep and excellence of artistic program that makes it dominate all else and virtually monopolizes attention.

The splendid tradition of collecting objects of virtu for the benefit of the general public proved an asset of great worth when minds turned toward the establishment of museums in the modern sense. But these did not come into being until the middle of the 19th century—later, in other words, than in many European cities. The reasons lie in the political history of Poland: the gradual erosion of her power in the 17th and 18th centuries and the eventual loss of independence. Although an imaginative plan for a public Musaeum Polonicum, roughly modeled on the British Museum and conceived in the spirit of the Enlightenment, was drawn up in 1775, its execution was overtaken by the fall of the state and so had to be shelved indefinitely.

Cracow formed part of the Polish territory that fell to Austria in the Partitions, and it was here in the second half of the 19th century that circumstances became more propitious for reviving the idea of museum institutions, although their chief aim was now seen as patriotic, and not solely scholarly and educational. The more liberal political conditions in the Austrian-ruled part of the country made this a practical proposition. In 1850 the Cracow Learned Society opened a Museum of Antiquities devoted chiefly to archaeology and numismatics. And the collections of the Jagiellonian University Museum, the only one which had preserved any kind of continuity, were steadily enlarged. Then in 1868 the efforts of Dr. Adrian Baraniecki led to the opening of a City Museum of Technique and Industry, the object of which was to raise standards in design and the applied arts.

By this time there had come about such a revival of learning and art in Cracow, closely observed and widely supported by Poles elsewhere, that in 1876 it was decided to bring the Czartoryski Collection back to Poland from Paris and find a home for it in Cracow. The oldest antiquarian and art museum in Poland, this collection had been founded at the turn of the century in Pulawy, the seat of the Czartoryski family, and removed to Paris in 1831 to save it from confiscation after the defeat of the November Insurrection. The Cracow municipal council made available the building of the old Arsenal and here too were housed the library of old books and records accumulated by the Czartoryskis. There was thus formed an extremely important and internationally renowned center of Polish culture and learning, comprising prints, national relics, weapons and armor, and art objects of foreign as well as Polish origin, and a small but choice gallery of Polish and European painting.

But it was the opening in 1879 of the National Museum, the first public institution devoted primarily to Polish art, that marked the climax of this stage of endeavors in the museum field. This significant development was made possible by spontaneous gifts and contributions of Polish people in all three of the partition zones and in the various parts of the world to which the political diaspora had taken them, complemented by purchases of a more modest order. The collections grew very rapidly and soon made the Museum the biggest of its kind in Poland, its program being gradually extended to foreign art, handicrafts and antiquities. As insurance against interference by the Austro-Hungarian authorities, this national institution remained nominally the property of the municipality.

Needless to say, the program also embraced folk art which at that time was beginning to arouse increasingly widespread interest among scholars, connoisseurs and collectors. In view of the enormous requirements in this particular sphere, it was decided to turn over this material and the fostering of the culture and art of the Polish countryside to a separate Ethnographical Museum, founded in 1910, which eventually also took in European and more exotic fields.

When independence was restored in 1918, a new institution, The Wawel State Art Collections, was added to the existing museums of Cracow, with their records of national history, culture and art. The old royal castle had been redeemed by public subscription from the Austrian authorities prior to the recovery of independence, but the considerable wear and tear it had suffered, the alterations made for military purposes and the looting and vandalizing of its interiors required many years of costly restoration, which still continues. In the course of time the superb original furnishings and appointments of the royal apartments, the Crown Treasury and the Armory were reassembled, and over the years the main elements of the material on display have been further enriched.

The tragic catastrophe which overtook the whole of Polish culture during World War II brought all museum activity to a complete standstill for over six years and inflicted huge losses. Although Cracow escaped the devastation suffered by the majority of Polish cities, its art collections were ruthlessly looted by the Germans. Though some of this plunder was traced and recovered after the war, much of it, including paintings by Raphael and Brueghel

14

the Elder, the priceless contents of the "Royal Coffer" in the Czartoryski Collection, gems of goldsmith's art, rare handicrafts and part of a collection of Japanese art, was lost forever.

The rapid development of museums in the postwar period has brought, in addition to reconstruction and enlargement, the establishment of new institutions. As early as 1945 a City of Cracow History Museum was founded with the object of presenting the history and culture of a city occupying so exceptional a place in the national heritage. The nucleus of its collections was formed by the objects assembled since the end of the 19th century by the municipal archives: seals, plans, prints, views, and other such antiquities. Other new museums are primarily of local interest and of too specific a nature for inclusion in this publication. The time spent by Lenin in Cracow and the nearby health resorts of Bialy Dunajec and Poronin is commemorated by a museum named after him. The Cracow Medical Academy has organized a Pharmacy Museum whose material, running to several thousand items, is for the moment available only to researchers. Finally, there is an Aviation Museum with records illustrating the history of Polish aviation in the years 1919–39.

The richness and variety of the art collections in Cracow have not only made its museums preeminent in Poland, but also mark them out among their counterparts in Europe as a whole. Their staffs include experts of international reputation in many fields, and their resources are drawn upon by the organizers of all major displays of the world's cultural and artistic heritage. The same applies, of course, to the exhibitions of Polish art periodically shown throughout the world. The continuous, carefully planned enrichment of Cracow's museum collections keep bringing to light splendid new values, of which this book can offer only a small, though tantalizing sample.

POLISH AND EUROPEAN ART
IN CRACOW COLLECTIONS

SWABIA or LOWER LORRAINE. *Wloclawek Drinking-bowl.*

Cast in silver, this drinking-bowl was undoubtedly originally a liturgical chalice. The four round medallions on the cup and the intervening triangular spaces show eight scenes from the story of the deliverance of the Israelites from Midianite bondage by Gideon, according to the Old Testament *Book of Judges*, Chapters VI and VII.

The unusual shape of the vessel, the archaistic composition of the scenes, the costumes, armor and weaponry, and the style of the ornamentation have given rise since its discovery to many different hypotheses as to its date and place of origin. A Polish art historian, Piotr Skubiszewski, has concluded that it was made in Western Europe in the third quarter of the 10th century (though some scholars have opted for as late as the 12th century), in the area between Swabia and Lower Lorraine. It may have been partly modeled on a similar Armenian artifact of the 9th century which shows influences of Persian art.

In that case the vessel would probably have been brought to Poland by early missionaries (Benedictines?) at the turn of the 10th and 11th centuries following the adoption of Christianity in 966. At a time and in circumstances unknown it was buried near a Reformati monastery in Wloclawek, where it was unearthed by a ploughman in 1909.

WORKSHOP OF THE VISEGRAD GOSPEL BOOK. *King David with Christ on His Lap* and *St. Luke the Evangelist.*   pp. 20, 21

The baptism of Prince Mieszko I in 966 led to the adoption of Western culture and Christian art in Poland. In the plastic and pictorial arts this process took place at first through the importation of the objects and works needed in religious worship, but by the time of the Romanesque period local centers were already thriving.

The Gospel Book, also known as the "Golden Codex of Pultusk"—*Codex Aureus Pultoviensis*—is the most precious of a small number of early Romanesque illuminated manuscripts brought to Poland, in all probability by Judith, daughter of Vratislav II of Bohemia, who married Prince Wladislaus I Herman (1079–1102) c. 1078. Judith presented it to the cathedral in Plock, whence it came to the collegiate church in Pultusk.

The Gospel Book comprises an evangelistary with pericopes for the whole year, canon tables, nine full-page canonical compositions, seventeen figural miniatures, three large initials and several dozen smaller ones.

The central medallion on this gold-ground page shows Christ sitting on the knee of King David, supported by two angels. The remaining four medallions represent the Evangelists, and among the miniatures in the Gospel Book they are remarkable for their monumental style.

St. Luke at his writing table, like the other three Evangelists on other pages, is shown seated in an animated pose, framed by a variety of stylized architectural motifs. The rhythm of the composition of some of the miniatures, the hieratic figural style, the color range restricted to muted reds, greyish blues and greens frequently interspersed with liberally applied gold, and the iconography indicate links with three other gospel books—at Visegrad, Gniezno and the Cathedral of St. Vitus in Prague—all of which have long been attributed to the Prague scriptorium, which in turn was influenced by Bavarian models (Regensburg). Because of the iconographic similarities of the codices it is thought that they were made according to some richly illus-

SWABIA OR LOWER LORRAINE
3rd quarter 10th century
Wloclawek Drinking-bowl
Silver, partially gilded, engraved and chased;
height 10.8 cm., diameter 15.5 cm.
National Museum, Cracow.

WORKSHOP OF THE VISEGRAD
GOSPEL BOOK
4th quarter 11th century
St. Luke the Evangelist
Parchment, 35.3 x 25 cm.
Czartoryski Collection,
National Museum, Cracow.

trated model whose illuminations were treated with minor variations in each of the four examples mentioned here. The Pultusk codex dates from the second half of the 11th century.

MEUSE SCHOOL (?). *Cross of Diadems.* *pp. 22, 23*
Two diadems of pure gold from the 2nd quarter of the 13th century—originally associated with Boleslaus the Shy, Duke of Cracow (1226–79), and his wife, the Blessed Kinga (1234–92), daughter of Bela IV of Hungary—were joined together during her lifetime and made into a cross. In the course of repairs in the second half of the 15th century, escutcheons with the coat-of-arms of Jan Rzeszowski, Bishop of Cracow (1472–88), the crest of the

Left and detail right
MEUSE SCHOOL (?)
2nd quarter 13th century
Cross of Diadems
Gold-plated wood, pearls,
precious stones, enamel.
83.5 x 58 cm.
Cathedral Treasure-house, Cracow.

Chapter of Cracow Cathedral and the Polish eagle were added to the base. The diadems are made up of rectangular links which in the horizontal diadem have pointed gables. Each contains enameled ornaments enclosed by open-work interlace into which are set figures of footmen, knights on horseback and fantastic birds, to which are added precious stones and pearls.

The date and provenance of the diadems is a subject of scholarly debate. Some art historians attribute them to the Meuse School, this region being one with which Poland maintained lively contacts in the 13th century; others think that they were made in Venice; more recently, a Hungarian origin has been advanced. The closest analogy to the Cracow diadems is the crown on the reliquary of St. Sigismund (1370) at Plock Cathedral, for the ornamentation of which a silver and gilded crown from the 13th century was used, the style bearing marked similarities to the Cracow diadems, despite the alteration made in 1601. They belong to the type of crown worn by Byzantine princesses, and the decorative motifs and stylization of the birds were to be found in various European centers during the 13th century, which is one of the reasons for the differences of opinion as to their provenance.

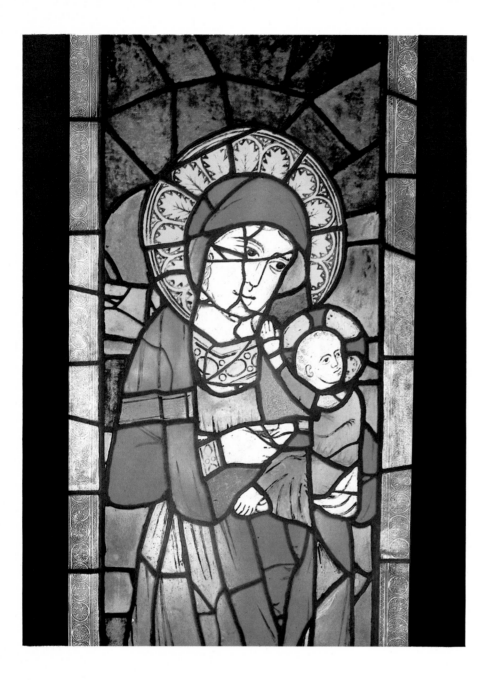

DOMINICAN MONASTERY WORKSHOP
End of 13th century
Virgin and Child, detail
Leaded glass, 88 x 52 cm.
National Museum, Cracow.

DOMINICAN MONASTERY WORKSHOP.   *Virgin and Child*, detail.
The Virgin and Child and two other stained-glass panels of similar size with
representations of St. Stanislaus the Bishop and St. Augustine, also in the
collection of the National Museum in Cracow, form part of a set of three
windows constituting the earliest surviving glass made for the Dominican
monastery in Cracow, which was brought from Italy in 1223 by Iwo
Odrowa, Bishop of Cracow.
The Virgin and Child group fills the whole panel, monumentally composed
with glass of saturated colors in which red, blue and green predominate. Although this glass has affinities with Italian work of the second half of the
12th century, especially Sienese, it is considered to be of local origin, com-
bining late Romanesque and early Gothic characteristics. In view of the
regular contacts, including matters relating to art, between the Dominicans

DOMINICAN MONASTERY WORKSHOP
First quarter 15th century
St. Mary Magdalen, detail
Leaded glass, 75.5 x 51.5 cm.
National Museum, Cracow.

in Cracow and the parent monastery in Italy the similarities of style may spring not only from the importation of finished products, but also from the work of monks versed in various branches of art who stimulated the advancement of crafts in Poland.

DOMINICAN MONASTERY WORKSHOP. *St. Mary Magdalen*, detail.

This stained-glass panel is one of seven with full-length figures of saints from the cloisters of the Dominican monastery in Cracow; their original setting, however, was without doubt the abbey itself. The figures in these panels stand out against a ground resembling patterned fabrics with foliate borders, under arcades composed of Gothic architectural elements. The *contrapposto* pose of the saint and the drapery of her cloak drawn with elegantly flowing lines in the manner of the courtly Franco-Flemish International Gothic style, testify to the skill of the medieval glass-painters of

WORKSHOP OF THE OLESNICKI
PONTIFICAL
Cracow, 2nd quarter 15th century
The Flagellation and Misericordia Domini,
c. 1430
Parchment, 30.7 x 22.5 cm.
Renaissance binding, leather over-boards,
blind- and gold-tooled.
Archives of the Metropolitan Chapter,
Wawel Hill, Cracow.

Cracow, who could boast a tradition reaching back at least to the 13th century.

Toward the end of the 14th century there was a blossoming of the art of stained-glass in Cracow which continued through the 15th, as indicated not only by the surviving windows in the churches of Our Lady and Corpus Christi, but also by the numerous references to glass-painters in municipal and guild records.

WORKSHOP OF THE OLESNICKI PONTIFICAL. *The Flagellation* and *Misericordia Domini.*

The Pontifical—or bishop's book of offices—contains forty-five miniatures and historiated initials. It was produced for Cardinal Zbigniew Olesnicki (1389–1455) in a Cracow illuminator's workshop, probably c. 1430.

Compared to Cracow miniatures of the first three decades of the 15th century, which followed the Bohemian School and International Gothic mod-

CRACOW PAINTER
Active 1st half 15th century
Epitaph of Wierzbieta of Branice, c. 1425
Tempera on wood, 91 x 74 cm.
National Museum, Cracow.

els of the turn of the century, the illuminations of the Olesnicki Pontifical reveal certain departures in the direction of realism which link them with Cracow panel-painting of this period and are evidence of the emergence of a local style of miniature painting in the course of the 15th century.

The Flagellation, which begins the canon of the mass in the Pontifical and is the most beautiful picture in the book, has been symmetrically composed on a sort of shallow proscenium backed by a flat wall richly decorated with rhythmically designed rosettes. Christ's two scourgers, burly figures with large heads and disheveled garments, are shown in dynamic postures. The composition of this scene resembles the illuminations in a Silesian manuscript from the workshop of Jan of Zytawa, and resemblances can also be discerned in its details with the paintings on the wings of a triptych in Kamionka Wielka. The illuminated initial below contains a representation of the *Misericordia Domini* Christ type, with the Olesnicki coat-of-arms next to it.

27

MASTER OF THE KRUZLOWA MADONNA
Active 1st quarter of 15th century
The Kruzlowa Virgin and Child,
early 15th century
Carved wood, polychromed, gilded, silvered;
height 118 cm.
National Museum, Cracow.

CRACOW PAINTER. *Epitaph of Wierzbieta of Branice.* *p. 27*

This is the earliest known example in Poland of panel painting of this kind. It commemorates Grzegorz (Gregory) Wierzbieta of Branice, steward to the royal household who died in 1425. He is shown as a knight in armor kneeling at the foot of the enthroned Virgin and Child, and is identified by two coats-of-arms and a Latin inscription. Branice is a village outside Cracow.

The idealized treatment of the Virgin's face and the soft drapery of her cloak are reminiscent of other examples of Malopolska (Little, or southern Poland) painting of this period, and these affinities make it clear that the author of the picture must have been a native of Cracow. He was obviously under the spell of Bohemian painting at the turn of the 14th–15th centuries, and these marked influences point south as another of the inspirations of Cracow painting. In the first half of the 15th century they were creatively transformed and developed into the original Little-Poland style.

MASTER OF THE KRUZLOWA MADONNA. *The Kruzlowa Virgin and Child.* *pp. 28, 29*

This sculpture, discovered toward the end of the 19th century in the parish church of Kruzlowa, a village southeast of Cracow, is the most beautiful representation of the Virgin carved in Cracow. Made for one of the local churches where it undoubtedly originally served as the centerpiece of a Gothic altar, its characteristic S-shape pose, the drapery falling down in vertical folds enclosing three herringbone festoons, and the lyrical, idealistic features, place the sculpture as the work of an anonymous local master following the International Gothic style prevalent in Central Europe around 1400.

The "Beautiful Madonna" type that emerged in stone sculpture in the second half of the 14th century under the influence of French art was continued in woodcarving into the 15th century in many countries of Central Europe. Models for the composition of the *Kruzlowa Virgin and Child* are to be found in the Madonnas of Bohemia and the sources of its style of drapery can be traced to Little Poland, Szepes, Silesia and even Bohemia and Austria. However, a comparison with Cracow art in and after 1400 reveals so many similarities that it can be regarded as the work of a woodcarver who developed a local, Cracow variant of International Gothic. Its date of origin has been tentatively placed between c. 1400 and 1420–30; the obvious resemblances to Little-Poland sculpture of c. 1400 strongly suggest that the Madonna of Kruzlowa was carved at a date nearer the beginning of the 15th century.

MASTER OF THE DOMINICAN PASSION. *The Flight into Egypt.* *p. 31*

This exponent of Late-Gothic realism in Cracow painting with recognizably individual features created a new canon of stockily proportioned human figures and introduced landscape to Cracow painting on a wider scale. His narrative style emerged from a creative synthesis of the established mode of the Cracow School and the achievements of European painting, especially Austrian. Around 1465 this artist executed twelve paintings on six panels for the high altar of the Dominican church in Cracow. Prior to the huge

altarpiece carved by Veit Stoss for the Church of Our Lady, the Dominican retable was one of the largest in medieval Cracow. It depicts scenes from the childhood and passion of Christ and from the life of the Virgin painted with great ingenuity of composition. This iconographic program, partly drawn from the Apocrypha, probably originated in the Dominican community of Cracow.

The highly graphic passion scenes, which seethe with villainous-looking figures, are contrasted with more epic-like panels showing episodes from the life of the Virgin and the childhood of Christ. In *The Flight into Egypt*—as also in the other scenes painted on the back of the panels—the artist replaced the raised gold grounds on the frontals with simplified and somewhat naive landscapes, a feature never before so prominently used in Cracow panel-painting.

The new elements in these pictures exerted an innovating influence on the art of Little Poland in the third quarter of the 15th century, which was also reflected in Szepes and Upper Hungary.

31

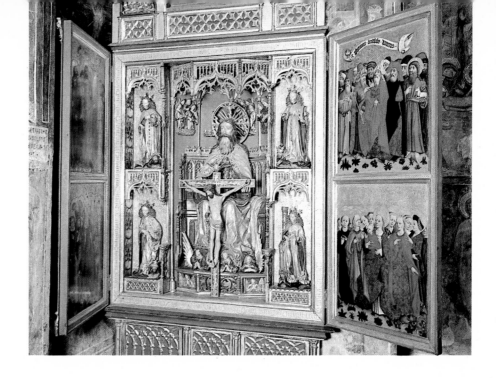

MASTER OF THE CHOIRS
Active in Cracow, 3rd quarter 15th century
Altarpiece of the Holy Trinity, 1467
Center panel: carved wood, gilded and poly-
chromed. Wings: paintings, tempera on wood.
Height (minus predella) 505 cm., width 406 cm.
Holy Cross Chapel, Wawel Cathedral.

Facing page
MIKOLAJ HABERSCHRACK
Active in Cracow 2nd half 15th century
Prayer in the Garden, c. 1468
Panel of altarpiece in the Augustinian church,
Cracow.
Tempera on wood, 124 x 103 cm.
National Museum, Cracow.

MIKOLAJ HABERSCHRACK. *Prayer in the Garden.*

In 1468, Mikolaj (Nicholas) Haberschrack, a painter and wood-carver active in Cracow in the years 1454–81, was commissioned by the Augustinian
Friars to make a retable for the high altar of their Church of St. Catherine
in the Cracow suburb of Kazimierz. The altarpiece consisted of a central
carved panel (which has not survived) to which were attached four lateral
panels, the inner leaves being hinged and painted on both sides, the outer
ones fixed and painted only on the front. The paintings show scenes from
the passion of Christ and the life of the Virgin and in this they bear a resemblance to the altarpiece in the church of the Dominicans painted a little earlier by the Master of the Dominican Passion. Haberschrack was a
contemporary of one of the foremost exponents of late-Gothic realism in
Cracow, namely the Master of the Choirs, whose figure types and, to some
extent, method of organizing pictorial space he adopted.

The author of the Augustinian altarpiece had a marked gift for variations of
mood. In the arrestingly dramatic *Prayer in the Garden*, which is set in a
nocturnal landscape beneath a dark blue sky, he caught the excitement of
the group of soldiers guided by Judas and contrasted it with the tranquillity
of the foreground depiction of Christ praying alone and the sleeping apostles, the olive grove moreover being painted with the precision of a miniaturist. At the bottom of the picture frogs crouch on the stony bank of a
brook spanned by a bridge, symbolizing the medieval concept of the demon-
ic world of the powers of evil. Affinities have been perceived in Haberschrack with Little-Poland artists—chiefly the Master of the Dominican
Passion and the Master of the Choirs—as well as analogies with broader
currents in Europe and, more specifically, Austria as represented by the
Master of the King Albert Altar and Master Schottenaltares in Vienna. The
details seem also to indicate a knowledge of Rhenish and even Venetian
styles. But whatever may be said about Haberschrack's links with Western
and local art, the original form of his works makes him one of the more
obviously individual artists of the late Middle Ages in Central Europe.

MASTER OF THE CHOIRS. *Altarpiece of the Holy Trinity.*   *pp. 33–35*
This eminent exponent of Cracow art in the late Middle Ages established a
new approach to landscape painting, gave an original shape to new iconographic ideas, and introduced a figure type with more homely features
which was adopted and repeated by other workshops in Cracow. Some art
historians have identified the Master of the Choirs with Jakub of Sacz, a
painter and wood-carver who also worked in Szepes and Slovakia.
The Holy Trinity altarpiece in Wawel Cathedral was probably endowed in
1467 by King Casimir IV Jagiello (1447–92) for the chapel of the Holy
Trinity (it was moved to the chapel of the Holy Cross in the 16th century)
either in thanksgiving for the victorious peace concluded with the Order of
the Teutonic Knights in Torun in 1466 or as a memorial to his mother,

MASTER OF THE CHOIRS
Active in Cracow, 3rd quarter 15th century
Choir of the Martyrs, 1467
Inside panel from wing of
Holy Trinity Altarpiece.
Tempera on wood, 103 x 83.5 cm.
Holy Cross Chapel, Wawel Cathedral.

34

MASTER OF THE CHOIRS
Active in Cracow, 3rd quarter 15th century
St. Eustace Hunting, 1467
Outside panel from wing of
Holy Trinity Altarpiece.
Tempera on wood, 103 x 83.5 cm.
Holy Cross Chapel, Wawel Cathedral.

Queen Sophia (d. 1461), the founder of this chapel in the cathedral. The central panel of the altarpiece consists of carvings of the Trinity, choirs of angels and four women saints, and the wings have paintings of apostles, martyrs, prophets and virgins adoring the Trinity. The backs of the wings show the *Conversion of St. Paul, St. Eustace Hunting, St. George and the Dragon,* and *St. Secundus Fording the River Po.* The top of the altar has carvings of the Resurrection, angels, St. Anne of Samothrace and St. Sophia. The subject matter, unique in the art of Cracow, was drawn from St. Ambrose's hymn *"Te Deum laudamus"* and an antiphon to the Trinity, the text of which is inscribed on the frame of the centerpiece.

Two different methods of organizing pictorial space are evident in these panels. The *Choir of Martyrs* on the front of the wings follows a traditional

Facing page
MASTER OF THE CHOIRS
Active in Cracow, 3rd quarter 15th century
Christ Sending Forth the Apostles, 1467
Center panel of triptych from church in
Mikuszowic.
Tempera on wood, 213 x 154 cm.
National Museum, Cracow.

local Gothic style: a crowd of saints with oval faces and prominent noses stand in shallow space on a narrow strip of ground. Above their heads is a flat gold background enlivened with an overall acanthus-leaf pattern. The hieratic rigidity of the figures is of considerable decorative value, recalling Stefan Lochner's well-known triptych in Cologne Cathedral, and suggesting influences of the Silesian Master of the King Albert Altar.

An entirely different treatment of pictorial space is found in the paintings of the knights on the back of the panels. *St. Eustace Hunting* is depicted in a landscape viewed slightly from above, having a high horizon and a screen of rocks and trees with paths running off in different directions. A walled city and snow-capped mountains are visible in the far distance.

New to the contemporary Cracow panel-painting are the panoramic landscapes, the variegated luminous greens, the skillful introduction in these open spaces of small figures usually shown in motion, and the relatively fantastic treatment of the architecture. Analogies with this innovative style have been sought in Austrian art and the Master E.S. But these distant affinities notwithstanding, there are many similarities with the painters of the Cracow school—such as the Master of the Choirs' contemporary, Mikolaj Haberschrack.

MASTER OF THE CHOIRS. *Christ Sending Forth the Apostles.*
The painting is the central panel of a triptych originally in Wawel Cathedral, but removed during the Baroque period to a church in the village of Mikuszowice near the town of Bielsko southwest of Cracow. It is the only representation in Polish art of this New Testament scene of the Apostles receiving their mission; the four Fathers of the Latin Church, St. Gregory, St. Augustine, St. Ambrose and St. Jerome, are shown on the inner sides of the wings. The Apostles are grouped around Christ standing on a rock and hold scrolls indicating the place where they are to preach the Gospel. A comparison of the Apostles in this panel with the *Choirs of Martyrs* on the wings of the Holy Trinity triptych in Wawel Cathedral reveals such close similarities in the construction of the figures, the drapery and the facial types that the author of the picture must surely also be the Master of the Choirs. The landscape style, with a high horizon and twisting paths winding between luminous hills among which can be seen a cluster of buildings, also points to the Master of the Choirs.

VEIT STOSS. *High Altar in the Church of Our Lady.* pp. 38–42
Veit Stoss, the greatest sculptor of the late Middle Ages, worked until 1496 in Cracow, where he was called from Nuremberg c. 1477 by the burgesses of the city to execute a huge retable for the high altar of the Church of Our Lady, which he completed in 1489. At the time of Stoss's arrival, Cracow was in every respect at one of the peaks in its development: girt by walls and fortifications, its Gothic churches already built and containing altarpieces painted and carved by local masters (some of them still preserved), their treasuries and sacristies filled with opulent liturgical furnishings, its Jagiellonian University thriving.

The high altar, made of linden wood, is one of the largest carved and painted pentaptychs in late medieval Europe. It consists of an arched centerpiece

p. 38
VEIT STOSS
Horb-on-Neckar c. 1448—Nuremberg 1533
High Altar in the Church of Our Lady, 1477–89
Linden wood, polychromed, gilded;
c. 1300 x 1100 cm.
Church of Our Lady, Cracow.

flanked by double tripartite wings, the hinged inner panels with bas-reliefs on both sides, the outer ones fixed and carved on only one side. Above it there is an openwork baldachin, of which only the section above the center-piece is still preserved. The lower part of the shrine displays the *Dormition of the Virgin* with monumental, larger-than-life-size figures of the twelve Apostles, one of whom supports the Virgin. Above this group, in a radiant halo surrounded by angels, is shown the *Assumption*. Scenes from the life of

Above and p. 40
VEIT STOSS
Apostles, details from the *Dormition of the Virgin*, centerpiece of the High Altar. Linden wood, polychromed; figures over life-size.
Church of Our Lady, Cracow.

39

Christ and Mary are depicted in the eighteen sections of the lateral panels, the *Tree of Jesse* on the predella, and the *Coronation of the Virgin* with angels and St. Stanislaus and St. Adalbert, in the baldachin.

The altarpiece in the Church of Our Lady is Stoss's greatest work. The powerful late-Gothic realism of the human figure (the details of heads, hands and feet are particularly eloquent) contrasts with the expressive and dynamic forms of the draperies which develop a life of their own, often with scant regard for the anatomy and posture of the human body. This contrast between the late-Gothic realism of the details of figures and the positively "abstract" expressionism of the draperies is what gives Stoss's style its remarkable power. His individuality set a stamp on the development of Polish sculpture in the late 15th and early 16th centuries, particularly in Cracow and in Little Poland in general, so much so that a considerable number of late-medieval wood-carvings justify the use of the term "post-Stoss." His influence was not, for that matter, confined to contemporary Poland, but can also be discerned in the art of Silesia, Slovakia and other areas which came within the artistic radiation of southern Poland.

VEIT STOSS. *Tomb of King Casimir IV Jagiello.* p. 43

Following the funeral of King Wladislaus the Short in 1333, Wawel Cathedral became in effect the necropolis of Polish rulers. At first the tombs themselves contained the remains of the deceased; later, as in the case of Casimir IV Jagiello, the sepulchral monument became only the outward symbol of the grave of the king, whose body was buried beneath the chapel floor.

The tomb of Casimir IV Jagiello was not commissioned by the king himself but by his consort, Queen Elizabeth; it was nevertheless executed during his lifetime. When he died in 1492, he was interred in a marble casket beneath the floor, above which a monument had previously been erected in the southwest corner of the Chapel of the Holy Cross. Like the other medieval royal monuments at Wawel, it takes the form of a sarcophagus with a high-relief effigy of the king lying on a heavy slab. It is surmounted by a canopy resting on eight columns. The slab is one of red Salzburg marble whose rich pattern of veins enhances the expressiveness of the carving. Only two sides of the sarcophagus are ornamented (the other two facing the wall of the chapel), and these are divided into four panels in each of which are carved in high relief two mourners displaying the coats-of-arms of Poland, Lithuania, Dobrzyn and Kujavia. The capitals of the columns supporting the canopy are carved with scenes from the Old and New Testaments. These are signed by Stoss's assistant, Jorg Huber of Passau. The sarcophagus itself bears the seal of Stoss with the inscription EIT STVOS 1492. Of supreme workmanship is the recumbent effigy of the king shown near death, with his head tilted back and a face suffused with pain.

The dramatic expression of the figure is heightened by the monumentally carved coronation robe whose hard, mail-like texture encases the body. The tomb of Casimir IV is the last medieval canopied monument of its kind in the cathedral. The last two kings of the Jagiello dynasty, who succeeded him, have tombs in a Renaissance style, marking a complete break with the design of this tomb. It is one of the most beautiful examples of late-medieval sepulchral art in Europe.

MARCIN MARCINIEC. *St. Stanislaus Reliquary.* *pp. 44, 45*

The inscription on the lid of the reliquary reads that it was endowed by Elizabeth of Habsburg (1436–1505), the widowed consort of King Casimir IV Jagiello, and her two sons who predeceased her, King John Albert (1492–1501) and Cardinal Frederic Jagiello. The commissioning of the reliquary was entrusted to Jan Konarski, who succeeded the latter as Bishop of Cracow.

Made of pure gold, the reliquary is in the shape of an octagonal, architecturally structured casket, a form frequent in the late-medieval goldsmith's work of Little Poland. The casket is supported by four angels carved in the round displaying the coats-of-arms of Poland, Lithuania and the Habsburgs

VEIT STOSS
Head of an Apostle, detail from the *Dormition of the Virgin*, centerpiece of the High Altar.
Linden wood, polychromed and gilded; figures over life-size.
Church of Our Lady, Cracow.

VEIT STOSS
Tomb of King Casimir IV Jagiello, 1492–94
Red Salzburg marble; 315 x 260 cm.
Holy Cross Chapel, Wawel Cathedral.

VEIT STOSS
Tomb of King Casimir IV Jagiello, detail
Red Salzburg marble.
Holy Cross Chapel, Wawel Cathedral.

(Elizabeth was the daughter of Emperor Albert II). It is covered by a flattened dome richly encrusted with precious stones. On the sides of the casket, beneath openwork canopies of exquisitely intertwined Gothic tracery, the goldsmith placed eight bas-reliefs with scenes from the life of St. Stanislaus the Martyr: *Purchase of the Village*, *Raising of Peter from the Dead*, *Testimony before the King*, *Murder of the Saint*, *Quartering of his Corpse*, *Eagles Guarding the Body of the Slain Bishop*, *Burial*, and the *Canonization* (which took place in Assisi in 1254). The canopies over each scene indicate that the goldsmith based their composition on the baldachins over the wings of the high altar in the Church of Our Lady carved by Stoss. The scenes, however, are less skillfully composed, with large figures lacking the dynamism and expressiveness associated with the art of Stoss. Nevertheless

Above and detail right
MARCIN MARCINIEC
Cracow goldsmith of turn of 15th–16th century
St. Stanislaus Reliquary, 1504;
Cast and chased gold; precious stones,
including sapphire and black diamonds.
Height 24.3 cm., diameter 31.6 cm.
Cathedral Treasure-house, Cracow.

44

their inspiration is clearly visible in the artistry of what is the outstanding example of late-Gothic goldwork in Poland.

On the inside bottom of the reliquary, the author engraved the inscription MARTINUS MARCZINECZ AVTHOR HVIVS OPERIS and on the lid he placed the date 1504 next to the founder's name. Marciniec, whose name appears in the records of the Cracow Goldsmiths' Guild from 1486 to 1518, was the foremost Polish master of this craft in the late Middle Ages. As official goldsmith to the court, he executed many royal commissions of which this reliquary is his masterpiece. The restraint and clarity of the ornamentation make it outstanding in the goldwork of late-medieval Europe.

CRACOW GOLDSMITHS' WORKSHOPS AND MARCIN MARCINIEC. *Sceptres of the Rectors of Jagiellonian University.*

Jagiellonian University, the oldest in Poland and the second oldest in Central Europe—next to Charles University in Prague—was founded in 1364 by King Casimir the Great (1333–70). Revived and reorganized in 1400 by King Wladislaus Jagiello and Queen Jadwiga along the lines of the University of Paris, it fulfilled for centuries the purpose for which it had come into being: the country's sole secular center of learning and source of an educated class. The high standards represented by its teachers, a tradition of freedom in propagating truth, tolerance and courage in embracing new ideas and beliefs brought renown to the University abroad and attracted scholars and students from many parts of Europe, a particularly large number coming in the 15th and 16th centuries from Hungary, Bohemia and the neighboring provinces of Germany.

These sceptres, which symbolize the authority of the University's heads, are carried before them on ceremonial occasions, and these three Gothic examples, made of silver and either entirely or partially gilded, are among the oldest preserved sceptres of European universities. Undoubtedly the work of Cracow craftsmen, they are considered the most splendid products of the goldsmith's art in late-medieval Poland. The sceptre on the left in the illustration comes from the late 14th century and was donated to the University c. 1400 under the will of Queen Jadwiga who died in 1399. On the inside of the crown is engraved the coat-of-arms of Wielkopolska (Great Poland, the region centered on the city of Poznan in western Poland) to which were added, doubtless in the 15th century, nine shields with the coats-of-arms of Poland, Lithuania, the House of Anjou (from which Queen Jadwiga was descended), the dukedom of Sandomierz, and of five dignitaries associated with the reinstatement of the University in 1400. It is probably the oldest preserved sceptre of its kind in the world.

The next sceptre (on the right in the illustration) was made in Cracow and—according to the inscription on the shaft—was bequeathed to the University in 1454 by Cardinal Zbigniew Olesnicki (d. 1455) who, as Bishop of Cracow, was also a governor of the University. The escutcheons with the papal coat-of-arms, the four-quarter armorial bearings of Poland and Lithuania, and the blazon of the donor engraved on the inside of the crown, also the four shields with the coats-of-arms of Poland, the Cardinal, and Lower Austria (the fourth is empty) on the underside of the top of the sceptre indicate that it was presented to Olesnicki as an emblem of the office of cardinal in 1454 by King Casimir Jagiello and Elizabeth of Habsburg who became

46

CRACOW GOLDSMITHS' WORKSHOPS and MARCIN MARCINIEC
Sceptres of the Rectors of Jagiellonian University.
Left, donated by Queen Jadwiga, c. 1400. Silver, gilded; length 110.6 cm.
Right, donated by Cardinal Zbigniew Olesnicki, 1454.
Silver, gilded; length 115.9 cm.
Center, donated by Cardinal Frederic Jagiello, 1493–5. Made by Marcin Marciniec.
Silver, gilded; length 108 cm.
Jagiellonian University Museum, Cracow.

his queen on 10 February 1454.

The third sceptre (center), artistically the most magnificent and originally also a cardinal's, is probably the work of the eminent Cracow goldsmith, Marcin Marciniec. It was made between 1493 and 1495 for Queen Elizabeth, who presented it to her youngest son, Cardinal Frederic, who bequeathed it to the university upon his death in 1503. This and the Olesnicki sceptre are the only two known European examples of such cardinal's insignia becoming emblems of university office.

MASTER OF THE POLYPTYCH OF ST. JOHN THE ALMONER.
Miracle after the Death of the Saint.

In the years 1496–1509 two Cracow painters, Jan Goraj and Joachim Lib-naw (who came from Droszowo in the west of Poland), worked in the church of St. Catherine in Cracow, from which this altarpiece comes, and attempts have been made to identify them with the anonymous Master of the Polyptych of St. John the Almoner, who is the first notable exponent of early-Renaissance painting in Cracow. The polyptych—which was painted c. 1504—comprises a centerpiece depicting a huge figure of St. John distrib-uting alms to assembled beggars, two inner leaves each the width of the centerpiece, with episodes from the life of the saint, and two narrow outer wings with scenes from the lives of the hermits of the Eastern Church.

This rare example in Polish art of a representation of St. John the Almoner, a 7th-century patriarch of Alexandria, can be attributed to the circum-stances attending the origin of the polyptych. Mikolaj Lanckoroński, who endowed the altar, traveled in 1501 on a diplomatic mission to Constantino-ple. Breaking his journey in Hungary where he was introduced to a cult of the relics of St. John the Almoner which Matthias Corvinus, King of Hun-gary, had reclaimed from the Turkish Sultan Bayazed, Lanckoroński was so fascinated with the culture of the East that he proceeded to commission the polyptych.

48 The painter skillfully combined the tradition of medieval Cracow paint-

MASTER OF THE POLYPTYCH OF
ST. JOHN THE ALMONER
Active in Cracow beginning of 16th century
Miracle after the Death of the Saint, c. 1504
Panel from wing of an altarpiece,
Tempera on wood, gilded; 104 x 121 cm.
National Museum, Cracow.

GEORGIUS
Active in Cracow, 1501–20
The Annunciation, 1517
Tempera on wood, 145 x 104 cm.
Czartoryski Collection,
National Museum, Cracow.

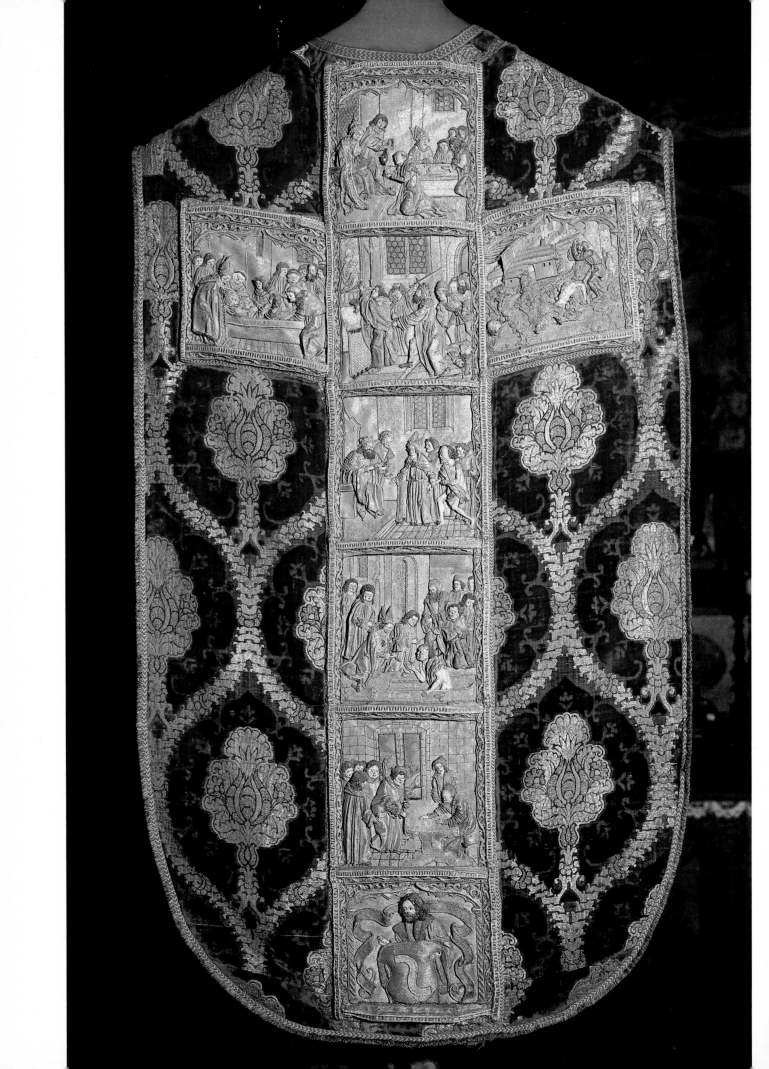

Left and detail above
CRACOW EMBROIDERER
Active early 16th century
*Chasuble with Scenes from the Life of St.
Stanislaus,* c. 1504;
Dark-cerise brocade with gold-thread pattern;
panels modeled in relief with gold thread, lamé,
pearls, lace; 140 x 82 cm.
Cathedral Treasury, Cracow.

ing—conventional perspective, a gold ground with engraved ornament, and drapery with harsh folds—with the new forms in art, these being apparent in the epic elaboration of the scenes from the life of the saint. Some of them are set in semi-fantastic landscapes painted by a perceptive observer of nature. Others, like *The Miracle after the Death of the Saint* in which St. John rises from his sepulchre at the request of a pious widow in order to give her a document testifying to her innocence, are shown with a perspective treat-

51

ment of the interiors and views of further rooms in the background suggesting the influence of Netherlandish painters. Another impressive feature is the narrative richness of the different scenes in which the figures have strongly characterized expressions and are dressed in sumptuous garments in the height of contemporary fashion.

WAWEL ILLUMINATORS' WORKSHOPS and MASTER OF THE BEHEM CODEX
Te Deum Laudamus: Enthronement of the King,
c. 1510
Pontifical of Erazm Ciolek
Parchment, 31.8 x 22.9 cm.
Czartoryski Collection,
National Museum, Cracow.

GEORGIUS. *The Annunciation.* p. 49

Painted in luminous, saturated colors, this Annunciation reveals the mastery of an artist delighting in realistic depiction. But concern for accuracy of detail has not blinded him to the needs of the composition as a whole, which testifies to a considerable grasp of the construction of figures modeled on the woodcuts of Dürer in the spirit of the new Renaissance art that was seeping into Cracow painting in the early 15th century despite the conservatism of its guilds. Although the donor of the picture is shown kneeling in the traditional posture of adoration at the feet of the Archangel Gabriel, the characterization of his face has the stamp of a modern portrait. Another new sign of the emergence of a type of awareness differing from the medieval is the date 1517, and a signature in the form of the letter G (for Georgius) inscribed on the insignia of the painter's guild painted above the capital of the column between the windows.

As regards pictorial content, the traditional Annunciation scene has been enriched with motifs intimating the Passion of Christ. On the pearl-embroidered stole of the Archangel can be seen lines from a hymn sung on Good Friday, while the Infant Jesus floating down on the golden rays above the Virgin's head is carrying a cross.

The picture is part of the centerpiece of a triptych executed for the collegiate church of St. Michael at Wawel, and the wings are now in the church of the Holy Cross in Cracow.

CRACOW EMBROIDERER. *Chasuble with Scenes from the Life of St. Stanislaus.* pp. 50, 51

Unlike decorative textiles which were in general imported in medieval Poland, embroidery was of local origin. In the early days of the Gothic style it was mainly modeled on panel painting; in the final period, the great flowering of sculpture in the 15th century led it toward various forms of relief.

Among the outstanding examples in Poland of raised, sculpturally modeled embroidery is this chasuble with scenes from the life of St. Stanislaus, presented to Wawel Cathedral at the beginning of the 16th century by Piotr Kmita the Elder, Voivode of Cracow.

The chasuble is made of brocade, probably Venetian from early in the second half of the 15th century, of dark cerise, double-pile velvet with a pattern of pomegranate flowers enclosed in pointed ovals woven in gold thread. On the back of the chasuble (shown here) there is a large embroidered cross consisting of eight squares, seven of which depict events in the life and cult of St. Stanislaus, while the eighth and lowest has a man-at-arms holding an escutcheon, a cross and a scroll with a now illegible legend referring to the donor of the chasuble. All the squares are decorated with great precision with embroidery of richly varied stitch. The ornamentation of the frames of each scene, the hems of the garments worn by the figures and other details are studded with pearls. The details of the embroidery—sword, chalice and

paten, thurible, pastoral, talons of eagles—are exquisitely worked in silver and then sewn into place.

The composition of the scenes, the modeling of the figures, and the richness and variety of the drapery indicate the hand of a consummate artist thoroughly familiar with late 15th-century Cracow sculpture, especially the work of Veit Stoss. Some art historians have tentatively identified him with Stanislaw Stoss, the son of the carver of the great altarpiece in the Church of Our Lady, who was active in Cracow in the years 1505–27 and was an officer of the sculptors' guild.

ILLUMINATORS' WORKSHOPS AT WAWEL and MASTER OF THE BEHEM CODEX.

Te Deum Laudamus: Enthronement of the King. *p. 53*

In the Middle Ages Wawel Hill, as the seat of government, the royal court and the diocese of Cracow, naturally had a number of scriptoria, and the groups of miniaturists associated with them produced a great many illuminated codices, some of them supreme examples of this art in Poland. These anonymous artists, whose identities were possibly concealed behind the various initials discovered on their miniatures, included the Master of the Behem Codex—the illustrator of a book of Cracow privileges and charters, and of the oaths and statutes of the city's guilds—and the Master of the Jasnogora Missal who illustrated for Erazm Ciolek, Bishop of Plock (1503–22), a Pontifical, or book containing the texts and prayers spoken by a bishop during the rites and sacraments described in the Codex.

The illuminations in the Codex were painted c. 1510 or in the following decade. Erazm Ciolek (1474–1522) came from a burgher family of Cracow. His natural ability and the education he acquired at Jagiellonian University raised him to a position of considerable prominence in the realm and, as secretary of King Alexander Jagiello (1501–06), he traveled on a number of diplomatic missions to Italy and Germany. He was also a leading patron of the arts and a bibliophile.

Among the features that set his Pontifical apart from Western European examples and three earlier Polish specimens (those of Zbigniew Olesnicki, c. 1430, Tomasz Strzempinski, 1455–60, and Frederic Jagiello, 1499) is that the texts relating to the ceremonial for coronations of Polish kings come first, preceding the forms for ordinations and consecrations.

The *Ordo Coronandi Regis Poloniae* in Ciolek's Pontifical was based on earlier medieval texts, most probably contained in the Pontifical of Cardinal Frederic Jagiello, while the origins of both lie no doubt in MS 17 in the Archives of the Wawel Chapter, entitled *Modus coronandi regem*, written for the coronation of Wladislaus III in 1434.

The *Ordo Coronandi* part of the Pontifical is illustrated with two miniatures, one smaller, occupying half the page and showing the actual coronation of the king, the other full-page and representing a scene entitled *Te Deum laudamus: Enthronement of the King*, which shows the moment in which the king, after his coronation, takes his seat upon the throne, while the populace, dignitaries and performers of the pageant attending the ceremony sing the *Te Deum*.

The composition of the picture space, its strict, though unpedantic axiality, and the perspective treatment of the scene within the frame of a late-Gothic portal are evidence of the author's familiarity with the designs of similar paintings in French and Dutch illumination that began to appear in the ear-

WORKSHOP OF MACIEJ OF DROHICZYN (?)
c. 1484–1528
The Woman Clothed with the Sun,
Adored by King John Albert,
early 16th century
Gradual of John Albert, Part III
Parchment, 74.5 x 52 cm.
Czartoryski Collection,
National Museum, Cracow.

ly 15th century. However, the manner in which the different groups and persons taking part in the rite are presented and their brightly colored dress—which combines features of Western and Eastern fashions—seem to link this miniature with the pictorial decoration of other Cracovian codices of the early 16th century and indicate that its style was drawn from local sources. The interpretation of its content recently advanced by Barbara Miodonska, a Polish art historian, makes the point that in the representation of an event as historic as the enthronement of a king, the artist's commission must obviously have included a statement of the idea then current that the authority of kings had a divine dimension. The intellectual profundity of the miniature as well as its artistic value place it among the most consummate works of central-European illumination as the Middle Ages were entering the modern era.

WORKSHOP OF MACIEJ OF DROHICZYN (?). *The Woman Clothed with the Sun, Adored by King John Albert.*
The illuminator was active in Cracow at Wawel, where he resided with the vicars of the Cathedral and doubtless was in charge of a workshop whose products included a Gradual executed for King John Albert (1492–1501) as

Above left
MASTER OF THE BEHEM CODEX
Tanner, 1505
Page in the Behem Codex.
Parchment, 17.6 x 14 cm.
Jagiellonian Library, Cracow.

Above
MASTER OF THE BEHEM CODEX
Cobbler, 1505
Page in the Behem Codex.
Parchment, 17.6 x 14 cm.
Jagiellonian Library, Cracow.

a gift for the Cathedral.

The gradual is a liturgical book containing the musical portions of the Mass sung by the choir, and the Gradual of King John Albert consists of three parts: *I. Proprium de tempore*; *II. Proprium de sanctis*; and *III. De Beata Maria Virgine*. It was copied in the years 1499–1506 in a Wawel scriptorium by Stanislaw of Buk, known also as Stanislaw of Wieliczka, and another scribe named Tomasz.

The first part of these huge codices, completed in 1501, contains the texts and notes of the masses for Sundays and the Lord's Days, i.e., Christmas, Easter and the feasts following Pentecost; the second part for other feasts, and the third for masses of Our Lady, votive masses and the Mass of the Dead. The style of the miniatures in the first two is on the conservative side with a predominance of flat colors and the broken line of late-Gothic drawing. The compositions show the influence of the conventions of graphic art. The Introit *Salve Sancta Parens* in the third part of the Gradual, which is more modern and innovative in style, begins with this historiated initial S containing a scene of the Virgin and Child being adored by King John Albert. The composition is reminiscent of the representation of St. John on the island of Patmos, his place in this miniature being taken by the kneeling king with the White Eagle at his feet, and the Virgin is shown as *The Wom-*

an *Clothed with the Sun* (*Mulier Amicta Sole*) of the Apocalypse, one of the most widespread Mary-types in the Middle Ages. In the Gradual the miniature served as a devotional picture in which the monarch entrusts himself and his kingdom to her care. The illuminations in this codex are not only remarkable for the depth of their religious feeling, but also illustrate the medieval concept of the divine right of kings.

MASTER OF THE BEHEM CODEX. *Painter, Tanner, Cobbler, Blacksmith* and *Tailor*. pp. 55–57

The Behem Codex is a book of 379 parchment pages recording the privileges and statutes of Cracow and the oaths and charters of its guilds. The first 274 pages were penned by Baltazar Behem, a Cracow townsman, Bachelor of Liberal Arts of Jagiellonian University, and a municipal scribe and notary in the years of 1500–08. The text was illustrated c. 1505 by a local painter with twenty-six miniatures relating to the city's guilds, with emblems and scenes of different trades. Aglow with brilliant colors and remarkable for the liveliness of their brushwork, they are the supreme achievement of Cracovian art, unfolding a vivid pageant of urban life at the end of the Middle Ages.

Though superficial borrowing of motifs from the early woodcuts of Dürer

and German book illustration are discernible, they have been transformed and adapted by the miniaturist to the requirements of his own style. On the other hand, a more obviously powerful source of inspiration for the realistic depiction of life in a late-medieval city is Netherlandish art. But even this does not swamp a style which clearly owes a great deal to the work of the Cracow miniaturist school. Most of the miniatures are enclosed in late-Gothic frames incorporating architectural motifs. Others are scenes showing a tanner and the emblem of a soap-maker composed as *tondi* contained in an ornamental square. The frames open onto vistas which can be divided into three groups. The first consists of interiors, mainly of craftsmen's workshops, which are vigorous studies of the life of Cracovian craftsmen with wittily observed genre features of considerable satirical edge. These are the best miniatures in the Codex. The second group comprises scenes set either in a landscape with streets running off into the background or with views of fantastic architecture blending into a blue horizon (*Tanner, Blacksmith*). The scenery is not that of Cracow or its environs, nor—in all probability—of any other specific city. The third group shows the blazons of guilds held by shield-bearers standing against a flat, usually monochrome ground.

The common feature of these groups is their composition, in which the principal figures are set in the foreground. They are dressed in Western European, Polish or Near Eastern attire (the latter was then fashionable in Cracow). The delicate or—in some of the pictures—slightly coarse hatching of the figures suggests that at least two painters contributed to the illustrations of the Codex. The anatomy of the bodies, the drawing of the hands and some of the heads and the perspective reveal here and there a certain roughness. On closer scrutiny, however, it becomes evident that many of the faces have a portrait-like accuracy; for instance, the tanner is an old man with a wrinkled face, and the bell-founder has a goatee. Irony is also evident in the depiction of the details of some occupations. For example, a cock standing on a shelf in the cobbler's workshop is clearly trying through his crowing to draw attention to the fact that the master's elegantly dressed wife in the foreground is flirting with a clown who is crouching in front of her. Again, the presence of a goat in the tailor's workshop alludes to the tale in which a practitioner of this trade was punished for stealing a customer's material by having to feed the latter's goat for a twelvemonth. The cards scattered at the feet of the tanner are a reminder of the guild's prohibition against gambling. These scenes indicate a familiarity with the plebeian literature then current in Europe, themes of which are reflected in the Codex.

The content and style of the miniatures in the Behem Codex testify to an efflorescence of art in Cracow in the transition between the Middle Ages and the Renaissance, a period in which the cheaper printed book with graphic designs was to supersede the elitist illuminated manuscript with its gems of miniaturist painting; yet, as can be seen from the Behem Codex, the art of illumination could still, even in its decline, give birth to works of entrancing beauty.

WORKSHOP OF LUCAS CRANACH
THE YOUNGER
Mid-16th century
Portrait of Queen Bona Sforza, Wife of Sigismund I
Oil on copper, 19.7 x 17.8 cm.
Czartoryski Collection,
National Museum, Cracow.

STANISLAW SAMOSTRZELNIK. *Portrait of Piotr Tomicki.* *p. 58*
Samostrzelnik was a Cistercian monk who lived in the order's monastery in the village of Mogile outside Cracow and was the parish priest of nearby Grocholice in the years 1513–30. The author of manuscript illuminations,

Facing page
STANISLAW SAMOSTRZELNIK
Cracow c. 1485—Mogila, near Cracow 1541
Portrait of Piotr Tomicki, 1530–35
Tempera on wood, 241 x 142 cm.
Cloisters of the Franciscan Monastery, Cracow.

mural decorations and paintings, he worked for the court of King Sigismund I (1506–48) and for the households of the Grand Chancellor of the
Crown, Krzysztof Szdlowiecki (as painter and chaplain), and for Piotr Tomicki, Bishop of Cracow. Of the numerous illuminated manuscripts attributed to his workshop, seven bear his signature. He may also have been the
author of the mural paintings in the church of the Cistercians in Mogile and
the portrait of Piotr Tomicki (1464–1535) painted between 1530 and 1535.
Tomicki, Vice-Chancellor of the Crown as well as Bishop of Cracow, was a

WORKSHOP OF LUCAS CRANACH
THE YOUNGER
Wittenberg 1515—Weimar 1586
Portraits of the Jagiello Family, c. 1556
Oil on copper, 19.7 x 17.8 cm.
Czartoryski Collection,
National Museum, Cracow.

humanist, patron of the arts and advisor to King Sigismund. He is shown here larger than life, dressed in pontificals painted in minute detail, standing in front of an arcade supported by candelabra columns and a half-drawn tapestry above which can be seen a patterned gold ground. Resemblances have been noted between the hieratic treatment of the Bishop and the representations of holy bishops in the Little-Poland school of late-Gothic altarpieces, while the candelabra and other details seem to be modeled on elements of Cracovian and German book design. The realistic,

HANS SÜSS VON KULMBACH
Kulmbach c. 1480—Nuremberg 1522
St. Catherine of Alexandria, 1511, detail
From altarpiece with scenes from the *Life of the Virgin*, painted for the Church of the Paulines, Cracow.
Tempera on wood; 56 x 38 cm.
Czartoryski Collection,
National Museum, Cracow.

forthright characterization of Tomicki's features places his portrait among the outstanding achievements of this branch of painting nascent in Poland in the early 16th century. Ever since its completion it has hung in the cloisters of a Franciscan monastery in Cracow where, from the 15th century onwards, portraits of the bishops of Cracow were painted, at first on the walls and subsequently on panels and on canvas. Tomicki's is the earliest surviving portrait in this gallery, which has been continued until the present day, and the first in which the subject's features were individualized, while its composition set the tone for subsequent portraits of bishops up to the late 16th century.

62

Facing page, top
MICHAEL LENTZ VON KITZINGEN
Franconian painter active in Cracow 1507–23
Martyrdom of St. Catherine, 1521
Panel from *Dormition of the Virgin*, triptych painted for Wawel Cathedral.
Tempera on wood; 110 x 83 cm.
National Museum, Cracow.

Facing page, bottom
HANS DÜRER
Nuremberg 1490—Cracow 1534 or 1535
St. Jerome, 1526
Tempera on wood, 41 x 31 cm.
National Museum, Cracow.

WORKSHOP OF LUCAS CRANACH THE YOUNGER. *Portraits of the Jagiello Family.* *pp. 59–61*

These miniature portraits of the family of the last two Polish kings of the Jagiello dynasty were painted c. 1556 in the workshop of Lucas Cranach the Younger, commissioned by King Sigismund II Augustus or one of his sisters. All bear the winged dragon—the mark of the Cranach workshop. Reframed in the 19th century, they can be identified as (from left to right, starting with the top row):

1. King Sigismund I (1467–1548), son of King Casimir IV Jagiello and Elizabeth of Habsburg, who ascended the throne in 1506 and was the founder of the Renaissance chapel of the Jagiellos in Wawel Cathedral and initiator of the conversion of the royal residence on Wawel Hill in the Italian-Renaissance style.

2. Queen Bona Sforza (1491–1558), Sigismund's second wife (whom he wed in 1518), daughter of Gian Galeazzo Sforza, Đuke of Milan, and an apostle of Italian culture at the Jagiello court.

3. Sigismund II Augustus (1520–72), son of Sigismund I and Bona, the last of the Jagiello line, who ascended the throne in 1548 and was a great patron of the arts and the originator of a monumental collection of tapestries commissioned in Brussels.

4. Elizabeth of Austria (1525–45), daughter of Emperor Ferdinand I, whom Sigismund II married in 1543.

5. Barbara Radziwill (1520–51), daughter of Jerzy Radziwill, Grand Hetman of Lithuania, who became Sigismund II's second wife in 1547 in romantic circumstances and against the wishes of the parliament.

6. Catherine of Austria (1533–72), daughter of Emperor Ferdinand I, and Sigismund II's third wife (1553).

7–10. The four daughters of Sigismund I and Bona: Isabella (1519–59), married in 1539 to John Zapolya, Duke of Transylvania and King of Hungary; Catherine (1526–83), married in 1562 to John III Vasa, Duke of Finland and King of Sweden; Sophia (1522–75), married in 1556 to Henry, Duke of Brunswick; and Anna (1523–96), married in 1576 to Stephen Bathory, Duke of Transylvania and King of Poland.

The realism of these portraits led to the belief long ago that they were painted either from life or from earlier full-length portraits, some of which have been found. In 1859 they were acquired for the Czartoryski Collection from the collection of Adolf Cichowski.

HANS SÜSS VON KULMBACH. *Catherine of Alexandria*, detail. *p. 62*

At the beginning of the 16th century Cracow—long established as the seat of government of a powerful kingdom, and having a renowned university and a wealthy bishopric—was a vigorous center of learning and art. In architecture and sculpture, the patronage of the kings of the Jagiello line introduced the new forms of Italian Renaissance art through the work of artists called from its homeland. In painting, however, the conservatism of the local workshops made them less receptive to these new currents. Nonetheless, partly through the support of Jan Boner (d. 1523), a banker and merchant who became burgrave of the city and was a loyal servant of the royal court, a group of painters from German cities came to work in Cracow and helped to propagate the new forms in this field as well. These art-

Facing page
MELCHIOR BAIER, goldsmith, d. 1577
GEORG PENCZ, painter, c. 1500–1550
PANCRATIUS LABENWOLF, bell-founder, 1492–1563
PETER FLÖTNER, sculptor, cabinetmaker, ornament designer, c. 1485–1563
The Silver Altarpiece in Sigismund Chapel, 1531–38
The altarpiece with shutters closed, showing the panels on the shutters and the fixed wings with scenes of the *Passion of Christ*, painted by Georg Pencz.
247 x 131 cm.
Sigismund Chapel, Wawel Cathedral, Cracow.

MELCHIOR BAIER
PANCRATIUS LABENWOLF
PETER FLÖTNER
Adoration of the Shepherds, 1531–38
Interior panel from The Silver Altarpiece.
Silver relief, partly gilded; 46.5 x 73 cm.
Sigismund Chapel, Wawel Cathedral.

ists were Hans Süss von Kulmbach, Michel Lentz von Kitzingen and Hans Dürer.

Kulmbach, also an engraver and glass-painter, came to Cracow from Nuremberg and between 1511 and 1516 painted altarpieces for the churches of St. Florian, Our Lady, and the Pauline Fathers in Cracow. *St. Catherine of Alexandria* was one of the panels of a triptych with scenes from the life of the Virgin painted in 1511 for the Pauline abbey. The other parts of this altarpiece are in different collections, the centerpiece, for instance, showing the *Adoration of the Magi* being in the Dahlem Museum in West Berlin. It bears the date 1511 and the signature of the painter, HK.

MICHEL LENTZ VON KITZINGEN. *Martyrdom of St. Catherine of Alexandria.* p. 63
This Franconian artist, active in Cracow from 1507 to 1523, was painter to the court of King Sigismund I until 1516 and then was employed by Jan Konarski, Bishop of Cracow. He left a numerous family in Cracow and was a member of the painters' guild. *The Martyrdom of St. Catherine of Alexandria* (1521) is part of an altarpiece showing the Dormition of the Virgin, painted for the sepulchral chapel of Bishop Konarski in Wawel Cathedral. A gifted eclectic, Lentz produced a synthesis of the styles of Lucas Cranach the Elder, Albrecht Dürer and Martin Schongauer, creating a work of great formal variety and considerable power. It stands apart from other Cracow painting of the time through its cold color scheme and the rich inventiveness in the construction of its different parts. Lentz exerted a certain influence on Cracow artists, who adopted some of his hallmarks—such as his type of landscape—without, however, really grasping the essence of the new elements in the work of this foremost exponent of the German-Renaissance style in Cracow.

HANS DÜRER. *St. Jerome.* p. 63

The younger brother of Albrecht Dürer, with whom he worked until 1510, settled in Cracow in 1527 where he became painter to the court of King Sigismund I. Among his works in Wawel Castle were the friezes along the tops of the walls of the royal apartments.

The *St. Jerome* was acquired by the Museum in the 19th century and is thought to have originated in Cracow. Its principal theme is in effect a wooded landscape painted with delicate brush-strokes and in part with very small dabs of color reminiscent of miniatures. The manner points to ties with the Danube school.

The picture is signed with the monogram HD and the date 1526, which has made it possible to identify a group of paintings also bearing this signature, akin in style to the Cracow painting and attributed to Dürer.

MELCHIOR BAIER, GEORG PENCZ, PANCRATIUS LABENWOLF, PETER FLÖTNER.

The Silver Altarpiece in Sigismund Chapel. pp. 64, 65

The Sigismund Chapel, known as a "gem of the Renaissance north of the Alps," is the work of an Italian architect. No direct antecedent has yet been traced for this beautiful chapel built onto the south side of Wawel Cathedral. It was erected in 1517–33 for King Sigismund I of the Jagiello dynasty who wished to have a mausoleum for himself and his family. The designer was Bartolommeo Berrecci, a Tuscan, who had been appointed royal architect and sculptor, and it was built of freestone, with a plan based on a square.

The elaborate decoration of the interior was the work of both local artists and others called to Cracow from various centers of contemporary Europe. Many of Sigismund's commissions for metalwork, goldwork and painting were placed in Nuremberg, and it was from this city that the authors of the altarpiece in the chapel were called. The altarpiece, executed in 1531–38, is a pentaptych with two hinged shutters, the entire interior of which consists of partly gilded silver bas-reliefs showing scenes from the Life of the Virgin and the figures of St. Stanislaus and St. Adalbert; the exterior of the shutters, and the fixed side wings are painted with 14 scenes of the Passion of Christ, his Resurrection and Ascension, by George Pencz. On the predella is the donor's plaque with the names of Sigismund I and Sigismund II Augustus.

The silver bas-reliefs were executed by Melchior Baier (d. 1577) on brass moulds cast by the goldsmith Pancratius Labenwolf (1492–1563) who worked from wood-carvings in low-relief by Peter Flötner (c. 1485–1546), the most gifted of this group of artists collaborating on the altarpiece. His compositions were to some extent based on the woodcuts of Albrecht Dürer's *Life of the Virgin.* Also active on the altarpiece was Hans Dürer— another Nuremberg artist then employed at the court of Sigismund I—who drew the plans for the recess in the apse of the chapel in which the altar was to be placed. Although the retable—which was already marveled at in the 16th century—is a product of Nuremberg art, the fact that it was commissioned by the Polish king and installed in the most magnificent Polish Renaissance building gives it a place in the history of art in Cracow.

BARTOLOMMEO BERRECCI
Vallombrosa (?)—Cracow 1537
or GIOVANNI MARIA PADOVANO
Active Padua 1515–1530—Active Cracow to 1553
Sepulchral Effigy of Sigismund I, 1529–31
Red marble, length 179 cm.
Sigismund Chapel, Wawel Cathedral, Cracow.

Pp. 68–69
BRUSSELS WORKSHOPS
3rd quarter 16th century
Tapestries of The Story of Noah in Senators'
Hall, Wawel Castle
Probably from cartoons by Michael Coxcie.
Wool, silk, gold and silver thread.
Wawel State Art Collections, Cracow.

BARTOLOMMEO BERRECCI or GIOVANNI MARIA PADOVANA.
Sepulchral Effigy of King Sigismund I.
The interior walls of the Sigismund Chapel—the most beautiful piece of
Italian-Renaissance architecture in transalpine Europe—are divided by Corinthian pilasters into tripartite triumphal arches surmounted by a deep
cornice supporting large lunettes on the axes of the arches, and flanked by
vaulted niches containing marble figures of saints, above which are bas-re-
lief *tondi* with busts of the Evangelists and the Old Testament Kings Solo-
mon and David. The surface of the wall panels and the drum of the dome
are covered with florid ornamentation, and the interior surface of the dome
is coffered with rosettes in relief. In the western arcade, on the right of the
entrance and facing the altar, stands a tomb monument with the reclining
figures of Kings Sigismund I and Sigismund II Augustus, on two registers.
The first was designed and carved in 1529–31 by one of two Italian artists—
Bartolommeo Berrecci or Giovanni Maria Padovana. This underwent alterations in 1574–75 when Santi Gucci, another Italian, raised the sarcophagus of Sigismund I to allow the effigy of Sigismund II Augustus to be fitted
into the lower compartment of the recess. The resulting structure set the
style for a type of two-tiered tomb which proliferated in Poland during the
Renaissance and Mannerist periods.
In contrast with the medieval tombs showing the effigies of kings in death,
that of Sigismund I, clad in stylized armor, is shown asleep, reclining on his

67

BRUSSELS WORKSHOPS
3rd quarter 16th century.
The Building of the Ark, mid-16th century
Tapestry from *The Story of Noah* probably from
cartoon by Michael Coxcie, with the marks of
Pieter van Aelst the Younger, Willem de
Kempeneer and the City of Brussels.
Wool, silk, gold and silver thread.
483 x 784 cm.
Wawel State Art Collections, Cracow.

side and supported on one elbow, and with his legs bent at the knees. This new mode of a sleeping figure in mortuary sculpture was linked with the ideas of Renaissance Neo-Platonic philosophy. The artistic form given to this belief in death as a state of slumber can be seen in Italy in the tombs of Cardinal Girolamo Basso and Ascanio Sforza in the church of S. Maria del Popolo in Rome. These are the intellectual antecedents of the tombs with sleeping effigies in European art, including that of Sigismund I. The specific feature in Poland is that it was the one country in Europe where this type of recumbent figure became a slavishly imitated formula.

BRUSSELS WORKSHOPS. *Tapestries of the Story of Noah in Senators' Hall, Wawel Castle.* pp. 68–77

The conversion of the medieval seat of the kings of Poland on Wawel Hill into a Renaissance residence was begun in 1502–06 on the order of Sigismund I, under an architect known as Francis the Florentine summoned from Hungary. He drew up the plans and introduced new architectural and sculptural forms in the style of the Italian Renaissance into the Gothic fabric of the Castle. After Sigismund had ascended the throne (1506) work continued in the north wing and was completed before the death of the Florentine in 1516 and the arrival in Cracow of Bona, daughter of Gian Galeazzo Sforza, Duke of Milan, to marry Sigismund. Following the wedding, work began on the east wing under Benedykt of Sandomierz, a Polish associate of the Florentine. In 1533, by which time another Florentine architect and sculptor, Bartolommeo Berrecci, was in charge, the completion of a screen wing on the south rounded off the conversion into a Renaissance palazzo. This consisted of a three-story building enclosing a pentagonal cloistered courtyard. Some tapestries for the interiors had been brought earlier from Antwerp and Bruges by King Sigismund I and Queen Bona; but it was their son, Sigismund II Augustus (1548–72), who commissioned from the most famous workshops in Brussels a collection of magnificent tapestries, of which 142 have been preserved in the Wawel collections. They were woven from wool, silk, gold and silver thread. In 1571 Sigismund II Augustus, the last king of the Jagiello line, bequeathed them to the Commonwealth, whereupon they were made part of the Crown Treasury and placed under the trusteeship of the Sejm (Parliament). But by the mid-17th century, following the war with Sweden, considerable inroads had been made into the collection, and from then until 1795, when it was removed to Russia, it underwent various vicissitudes, though always sooner or later returning to Wawel. The surviving tapestries were recovered following the Treaty of Riga in 1921 when the Soviet Union returned the Polish art treasures carried off by Tsarist Russia during the Partitions in the 19th century. In 1939 the collection was taken to Canada to prevent it from falling into the hands of the German invaders. It returned to Poland in 1961.

The tapestries were specially designed for the Wawel interiors and their dimensions tailored to the walls of the state apartments. Those which now hang in Senators' Hall with scenes from the story of Noah—*Noah's Conversation with God, The Building of the Ark, Boarding the Ark, The Flood, The Departure from the Ark, Noah's Thanksgiving, God Blesses Noah, The Drunkenness of Noah*—have been arranged according to the 1553 descrip-

72

BRUSSELS WORKSHOPS
3rd quarter 16th century.
God the Father and Adam, mid-16th century
Detail of *The Story of Paradise*, from
The Story of the First Parents, probably
from cartoon by Michael Coxcie, with the
mark of Jan de Kempeneer.
Wool, silk, gold and silver thread;
463 x 854 cm.
Wawel State Art Collections, Cracow.

P. 74
BRUSSELS WORKSHOPS
3rd quarter 16th century
The Stork-Gadfly, c. 1560
Tapestry in animal series, probably from
cartoon by Antwerp artist associated with
Pieter Coecke van Aelst, with marks of the
City of Brussels and Catherine van
Huldenberghe, widow of Nicolas Leyniers.
Wool, silk, gold and silver thread.
438 x 120 cm.
Wawel State Art Collections, Cracow.

P. 75
BRUSSELS WORKSHOPS
3rd quarter 16th century
*Otter with a Fish in its Mouth, Swans,
Storks and Fantastic Lizards*, c. 1560
Tapestry from the animal series, probably
from cartoon by an Antwerp artist associated
with Pieter Coecke van Aelst, with marks of
the City of Brussels and Jan van Tieghem.
Wool, silk, gold and silver thread;
395 x 261 cm.
Wawel State Art Collections, Cracow.

tion of the room contained in a panegyric written by Stanislaw Orzechowski for the marriage of Sigismund II Augustus and Catherine of Austria. They are among the most valuable works of art belonging to the original appointments of the Castle, and now comprise the following groups of tapestries: 1. Scenes from the Book of Genesis; 2. Landscape and animal motifs; 3. Coats-of-arms of Poland and Lithuania or the monogram (SA) of Sigismund Augustus; 4. Grotesque or landscape motifs. These were purchased from the workshops of Willem Pannemaker, Jan van Tieghem and Nicolaes Leyniers.

The cartoons for the Biblical series were in all probability drawn by Michael Coxcie (1499–1592), known as "the Flemish Raphael." The tapestries with landscapes and animals were woven c. 1560, probably from designs by an artist of the Antwerp Guild who may have been associated with Pieter Coecke van Aelst. The verdures of about the same date were the work of an artist from the workshop of Cornelis Floris and Cornelis Bos. The *Building of the Ark*, signed with the emblems of the city of Brussels and the workshops of van Aelst the Elder and Willem de Kempeneer, and the *God the Father and Adam* from *The Story of the First Parents* cycle signed by Jan de Kempeneer are good illustrations of the originality and beauty of the figural tapestries. The statuesque figures in the foreground dressed in richly draped garments or boldly shown in the nude—undoubtedly inspired by what Coxcie had seen in the work of Raphael—act out the story against Mannerist landscapes with meticulously detailed flora and touches of *staffage* ornament. The tapestries in this series, whose compositions show much concern with the problem of setting figures in a landscape, are among the finest examples of the Flemish tapestry-makers. This accounts for the fact that the Wawel motifs were still being repeated in commissions for other customers as late as the end of the 17th century.

The verdures with animals and landscape—a rare design in the 16th century—were executed in three different shapes depending on the place where they were to be hung. The *Leopard Fighting a Bear* is a horizontal oblong. The *Otter with a Fish in its Mouth, Swans, Storks and Fantastic Lizards* and *The Stork-Gadfly* are examples of elongated vertical rectangles; a third group consists of squares. The animals, real or imaginary, reposing or fighting, are shown, with all the zoological accuracy of contemporary knowledge, in settings composed in the style of northern Mannerism and its synthesis of Venetian landscape painting and the northern tradition. The vistas of forests with prospects between the trees of distant clearings and water-meadows skirted by hills on the horizon are among the earliest examples of the emergent northern Mannerist landscape and herald the subsequent landscapes of the Frankenthal School. Representations of animals in art have a very old tradition which in the 16th century converged with the awakening of interest in nature. The animals in the Wawel tapestries, apart from their symbolic and moralizing function, also served the purpose of imparting knowledge about the world of fauna.

A large group of the tapestries consists of ornamental compositions with grotesque motifs (pp. 78, 79). Some of them intertwine around the monogram of the king or the coats-of-arms of Poland and Lithuania. The grotesques in the Wawel tapestries are among the outstanding examples of this kind in northern Mannerism. Thanks to the richness and variety of their figural motifs, taken from classical mythology or the medieval imagination,

they possess a very interesting intellectual meaning. The tapestry with the royal monogram and a globe (p. 79), regarded as the most beautiful verdure with a Flemish grotesque design, shows a fanciful representation of the continents, intended by the designer to symbolize the power and glory of the monarch. The exuberant inventiveness of the grotesques has antecedents in

BRUSSELS WORKSHOPS
3rd quarter 16th century
Leopard Fighting a Bear, c. 1560
Tapestry from the animal series, probably
from cartoon by an Antwerp artist associated

with Pieter Coecke van Aelst.
Wool, silk, gold and silver thread;
147 x 329 cm.
Wawel State Art Collections, Cracow.

illustrated books current in the Netherlands, but there is no evidence of slavish imitation of stereotyped models. The commissioning of such an incredibly lavish set of tapestries to fit the exact measurements of certain interiors by a king of Poland testifies not only to his far-reaching taste, but also to the general standards of humanist culture in the country.

77

ANONYMOUS 16TH-CENTURY POLISH EMBROIDERER. *Binding of Queen Anna Jagiello's Prayerbook.* *p. 80*

The binding of the prayerbook of Queen Anna Jagiello (1523–96) contains two texts: *Parvus Mundus* by Haechtanus Laurentius (Antwerp, 1579) and *De deis gentium imagines* by Philippus Galleus (Antwerp, 1581). The book was donated by the queen in 1584 to the library of Jagiellonian University

BRUSSELS WORKSHOPS
3rd quarter 16th century
Cartouche with Royal Monogram SA Supported by Two Satyrs, c. 1560
Tapestry in the *Grotesques* series, from cartoon by an artist associated with Cornelis Floris and Cornelis Bos.
Wool, silk and silver thread; 239 x 219 cm.
State Art Collections, Cracow.

BRUSSELS WORKSHOPS
3rd quarter 16th century
Grotesque with Royal Monogram SA and Globe,
c. 1560
Tapestry in the *Grotesques* series, from
cartoon by an artist associated with
Cornelis Floris and Cornelis Bos, with
marks of the City of Brussels and
Catherine van Huldenberghe.
Wool, silk, gold and silver thread;
285 x 335 cm.
Wawel State Arts Collections, Cracow.

which was once housed in the Collegium Maius, its principal and oldest
building.

The front and back covers are of red velvet on which are embroidered two
Polish Eagles framed by an ornamental border. They also show the date
1582 and the initials AJ/RP (Anna Jagiellona Regina Poloniae). In view of
the techniques employed, the binding is classified under the head of embroi-

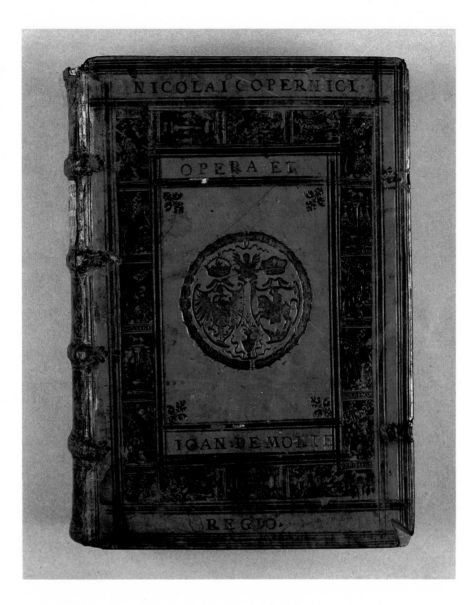

WORKSHOP OF JERZY MOELLER
16th-century Cracow bookbinder
Binding of the First Edition of Copernicus'
"DE REVOLUTIONIBUS ORBIUM
COELESTIUM," 1551
Dark-brown calfskin, blind- and gold-tooled;
29 x 30 x 5 cm.
Czartoryski Library, National Museum, Cracow.

dery. The clarity of the composition, the stylization of the eagles and the form of ornament point to a local workshop and thus testify to the high standards attained by the art of embroidery in Renaissance Cracow.

ANONYMOUS 16TH-CENTURY CRACOW GOLDSMITH. *Cockerel of the Cracow Bowyers' Brotherhood.* *p. 81*

The Brotherhood of Bowyers, also known on account of its emblem as the Cockerel Brotherhood, was one of the oldest townsmen's associations in Cracow (and survives to the present day). In bygone ages it served an important purpose in the defense of the city, training its members in the manual of arms and organizing annual marksmanship tournaments, the winner of which held the title of "Cockerel King" for the following year. The emblem of his reign was a silver cockerel stylized in the manner of an eagle, chased and partly gilded, standing astraddle on a support in the form of a bough. It is thought to have been donated to the Brotherhood in 1565 by King Sigismund II Augustus, a great patron of the arts, especially of the decorative kind. The slightly stiff late-Gothic modeling of the cockerel and

P. 80
ANONYMOUS 16TH-CENTURY POLISH
EMBROIDERER
Binding of the Prayerbook of Queen
Anna Jagiello, 1582
Red velvet, gold and silver thread, pearls,
corals and lazurite; 22.2 x 13.5 cm.
Jagiellonian Library, Cracow.

P. 81
ANONYMOUS 16TH-CENTURY CRACOW
GOLDSMITH
Cockerel of Cracow Bowyers' Brotherhood, c. 1565
Silver, partly gilded, enamel; height 42 cm.
City of Cracow History Museum.

the stylization of the crown, and the absence of a guild mark and the name of the craftsman seem to suggest that it was made in Cracow, where Gothic motifs survived alongside the new Renaissance elements in Polish goldsmith's work until the end of the 16th century and the municipal authorities did not yet insist on the stamping of gold and silver articles with special hallmarks. Because of the use for which it was intended, the cockerel is an unusual example of the goldsmith's art in Poland at a time when objects with a religious purpose predominated.

WORKSHOP OF JERZY MOELLER.
Binding of the First Edition of Copernicus' "De Revolutionibus Orbium Coelestium," 1551.   *p. 82*

Since the Middle Ages Cracow, as a seat of kings and bishops and a center of learning with a university founded in 1364, had been not only Poland's biggest importer of books, but also produced them on a large scale, in printed form from 1475 onward. The heyday of the bookbinder's art in the city was the 16th century when a number of workshops flourished, the largest of them working for the court. Sigismund II Augustus, the last ruler of the Jagiello line, was a passionate bibliophile, and one of the workshops which he commissioned in 1547–55 to make bindings for his imposing collection was that of Jerzy Moeller, a native of Silesia who acquired Cracow citizenship in 1529 and gradually established himself as the principal bookbinder to the court, a position he held until the 1560s.

The first edition of *Revolutions of the Heavenly Bodies*, which presented in full the epoch-making heliocentric theory of the great Polish astronomer, Mikolaj Kopernik (Copernicus), was printed in Nuremberg in 1543 and, together with the critical expositions by Regiomontanus and Peuerbach of the Ptolemaic system, was bound for the king in 1551. The binding displays all the characteristics of the Moeller style of binding at its height. The center of the front cover is occupied by the bookplate of the royal library in the form of a *tondo* with the coats-of-arms of Poland and Lithuania. The outer frame consists of a continuous strip of panels with scenes from the Old Testament. The back, which is composed of similar motifs, but without the bookplate, has the inscription SIGISMUNDI AVGVSTI REGIS POLONIAE MONVMENTVM 1551. Moeller's bindings are remarkable for the precision of their composition and their extremely skillful combination of tooling in blind and gold, features which place them among the outstanding examples of this art in 16th-century Poland.

ANONYMOUS 16TH-CENTURY POLISH PAINTER. *Portrait of Benedykt of Kozmin.*

Benedykt of Kozmin was a professor at Jagiellonian University and a poet who wrote in Polish and Latin. The son of a townsman of modest means in Kozmin Wielki in Great (western) Poland, he entered the university in 1520 and stayed there to teach classical Roman poetry, his special interests being Ovid, Horace and Virgil. In his own verse he displayed considerable felicity of language, though his style was heavily influenced by classical literature. Toward the end of his life he turned to theology and for some time was much in demand as a preacher in Wawel Cathedral. He bequeathed his collection of books and the portrait shown here to the university library and made an endowment for further acquisitions. He died in Cracow in 1559.

ANONYMOUS 16TH-CENTURY POLISH PAINTER
Portrait of Benedykt of Kozmin, c. 1550
Oil on canvas; 120 x 88 cm.
Jagiellonian University Museum, Cracow.

83

MARCIN KOBER
Wroclaw?—Zmarl 1600
Portrait of King Stephen Bathory, 1583
Oil on canvas; 226 x 122 cm.
Monastery of the Missionary Fathers, Cracow.

TOMASO DOLABELLA (?)
Belluno c. 1570—Cracow 1650
Portrait of Stanislaw Teczynski, before 1634
Oil on canvas; 195 x 108 cm.
Wawel State Art Collections, Cracow.

In the portrait the scholar stands beside a table, on which are symbolically placed a vase of carnations and an hourglass; and behind him hangs a curtain which divides a landscape background. The plaque at the bottom is a later addition. The style follows a formula for this kind of likeness that became current in the humanist world of Cracow in the second quarter of the 16th century, the influence of Italian art, largely assimilated via painters from southern Germany, being obvious. The contrast between the soft and realistic modeling of the face and the schematic and awkward delineation of the objects in the background makes it seem likely that the author was a guild painter with only a superficial command of the new language of art.

MARCIN KOBER. *Portrait of King Stephen Bathory.* p. 84

Marcin Kober was court painter to two Polish kings, Stephen Bathory and Sigismund III Vasa. He came to Cracow from Wroclaw c. 1583 and was later active in Prague and Graz where he was employed at the courts of Emperor Rudolph II and Archduke Ferdinand. He also traveled to other places, but continually returned to Cracow where he had a workshop managed during his absences by his wife Dorota and one of his journeymen, Marcin Teofilowicz.

The Portrait of King Stephen Bathory (1533–86)—Prince of Transylvania and King of Poland from 1575—is signed with the monogram MK and bears the date 1583. It shows the monarch in full length, dressed in a Polish-Hungarian costume against a symmetrically parted, dark green curtain. The statuesque, truly majestic pose of the king and the realistic delineation of his features (unquestionably drawn from life) make this one of the supreme achievements of Polish portraiture. Through its synthesis of western and central European styles of portraiture with local developments in this field, it became a model for many subsequent paintings of Polish kings and noblemen in the 17th and even 18th centuries, giving rise to a type known in Polish art history as the "Sarmatian portrait." The term derives from the efforts of the landed gentry at the beginning of the 16th century to trace the genealogy of the kind of state into which Poland had developed—a multinational monarchy dominated by the landowning class—leading to the formulation of an ideology which maintained that the Polish gentry was descended from the ancient tribe of Sarmati. This ideology formed the mold for a self-image of the gentry which survived into the 19th century and gave rise to the very original view of the world, culture and ethos current in Poland during the Baroque period. Sarmatism, as it was called, played an important part in giving a highly distinctive shape to Polish art in the 17th and 18th centuries.

TOMASO DOLABELLA (?). *Portrait of Stanislaw Teczynski.* p. 85

From the Venetian workshop of Antonio Vassilachi (Aliense), a pupil of Paolo Veronese, Dolabella came to Cracow c. 1598 and was engaged as court painter to King Sigismund III Vasa (1587–1632). In 1609, when the royal court moved to Warsaw, he stayed on in Cracow where he now had a home and family, and executed only occasional commissions for the king. His works included multi-figure religious compositions for a large number of monasteries and churches. To meet the flood of orders that came his way in the course of a career spanning over fifty years, he organized two work-

ANONYMOUS 17TH-CENTURY POLISH PAINTER
Portrait of Lucasz Opalinski, c. 1640
Oil on canvas; 202 x 132 cm.
Czartoryski Collection,
National Museum, Cracow.

LVCAS DE BNIN OPALINSKI.
SVPREMVS REGNI MARSCHA.
LEZ AYSC. KOSCIERZEN:SREMEN.
WALECEN KOLEN ODOLANOV:
KAMIONA LOSICEN RVBIESZOW:
VISCEN PILEN GIERANOW:
SIFMIEN METELEN WOLBRAM:
PREFECTVS

ANONYMOUS 17TH-CENTURY POLISH
PAINTER
Portrait of Stanislaw Biezanowski
Oil on canvas, 116 x 80.5 cm.
Jagiellonian University Museum, Cracow.

shops. Only a few paintings known from the records to be by him have survived. A typical representative of the declining phase of late-Renaissance Venetian Mannerism inspired by Tintoretto, Veronese and the Bassani, he exerted a strong influence on Polish painting in the second half of the 17th century. In his later work there are clear traces of Polonization. The *Portrait of Stanislaw Teczynski* (1611–34) shows the youngest son of Jan Teczynski, Voivode of Cracow, and his wife Dorota. He is wearing the Polish nobleman's costume of white *zupan* under a *delia* of the same color lined with brown fur, fastened with a row of studs and topped by a fur collar and, on his head, a calpac with feathers. The legend in the upper left corner is a later addition. The composition of the portrait and the pose of the subject show no departures from the convention that had become standard in Polish art from at least the end of the 16th century, but the masterful execution is such that it makes this painting one of the outstanding achievements of the second quarter of the 17th century in Poland. Some art historians have thought it the work of a Dutch or Flemish painter active in Poland; others, that it was produced by a native court artist. But the balance of opinion has favored a painter of north Italian origin, and more recently there has been a return to the theory ascribing it to Tomaso Dolabella.

ANONYMOUS 17TH-CENTURY POLISH PAINTER. *Portrait
of Lukasz Opalinski.*   *p. 87*
Lukasz Opalinski, Grand Marshall of the Crown (1574–1654), is depicted here in a typical Polish costume. The red, close-fitting *zupan* and a matching flared *delia* with a broad, dark fur collar and yellow knee-length boots are rounded off with a sword of a Polish-Hungarian type hanging from his left hip, a jeweled gold belt, and gold buttons on the *zupan* and the *delia*. In his right hand he clasps the emblem of authority, a studded and knurled black marshal's staff with a rhythmically repeated pattern of STs (the monogram of King Sigismund III of the Vasa dynasty) beneath the crown. The portrait belongs to the old Polish formal full-length type initiated by Marcin Kober's portrait of King Stephen Bathory (p. 84). Its typical features are a somewhat stiff pose, the use of monochromatic color schemes for the dress, and as realistic a characterization of the face as the painter's abilities permit. Great emphasis is laid on accentuating such accessories as symbols of authority or office which are supplemented by coats-of-arms and explanatory captions of the picture. Portraits of this kind, many of them also reduced to half-length, were produced on a mass scale in Poland during the Baroque period. What gives them an arresting quality is not only the exotic costume and details, but in particular the distinctiveness of the artistic values.

ANONYMOUS 17TH-CENTURY POLISH PAINTER.
Portrait of Stanislaw Biezanowski.
Biezanowski was born in 1628 into a burgher family in Lvov. In 1655, although already blind, he completed his studies at the university in Cracow and in 1689 was appointed its official chronicler. He was the author of a host of rhymed panegyrics written in a typically ornate Baroque style. By contrast the prose is more simple and succinct. Despite his infirmity, he was one of the most prolific writers of the Baroque period. The portrait shows

him with the typical appurtenances of the scholar, and is painted in a manner that had become established in Polish art in the 16th century. A characteristic not only of this particular example, but of Polish 17th-century portraiture in general, is the concern with capturing a realistic likeness of the subject. In the portrait of Biezanowski there is the added and moving touch of the unseeing eyes shaded by a green visor.

UNKNOWN 17TH-CENTURY POLISH PAINTER. *Coffin Portrait of a Young Woman, d. 1686.*

Coffin portraits are one of the original developments of Polish Baroque culture and have no counterpart in European art. The oldest known example is an oval likeness of King Stephen Bathory painted on a lead sheet in 1586, now in the Treasure-house of Wawel Cathedral. Coffin portraits were made on a mass scale in the 17th and 18th centuries. They were painted on copper, lead or brass supports, sometimes coated with silver or gold and usually of the same shape as the end of the coffin—that is, hexagonal, octagonal, oblong, square or, more rarely, oval. With few exceptions they show the head or the bust of the deceased, in most cases someone of noble birth, with eyes closed as in life, of healthy complexion (when shown in death the face is of a uniform pallor) and dressed in the fashion of the times. In the background there are occasionally identifying legends or letters and coats-of-arms. The authors of these pictures were by and large anonymous provincial artists, some of whom nevertheless achieved a degree of forthright realism in their portrayals which was far removed from Baroque panegyrics, and fell not far short of caricature in the way it laid bare the physical quirks and psychological foibles of the subject. No convincing explanation of the origin and popularity of this phenomenon in Polish culture has yet been advanced. All that is certain is that the coffin portrait formed part of the occasional decor ("*castrum doloris*") built for a funeral after which it was usually hung in the church or a sepulchral chapel. The portrait shown here is that of a young woman who died at the age of eighteen in 1686. The ornamentation of the French-style costume is matched by an equally rich array of jewelry consisting of chains, pearls and earrings.

JAN CHRYSTIAN BIERPFAFF. *The Capitulation of Sheyn at Smolensk in 1634*, c. 1648, detail.

The ornamental burial caskets of the kings of the Swedish Vasa dynasty who reigned in Poland from 1587 to 1668 were mainly made in the Commonwealth's two foremost centers of the goldsmith's art at this time: Gdansk and Torun. In the Middle Ages a separate crypt was excavated for each king under the floor of Wawel Cathedral and a slab laid over it. From the second quarter of the 16th century to the middle of the 17th they were buried in a single royal vault beneath Sigismund Chapel. When it was full, Wladislaus IV (1634–48) decided to build a new crypt underneath the Chapel of SS. Peter and Paul and it was here that he himself was buried in January 1649. Above it King John Casimir (1648–68) erected a chapel of the House of Vasa.

The casket of Wladislaus IV is made of wrought and fire-gilt copper and in transversal section is a hexagon. The sides are divided by four broad ornamental bands into rectangular panels at the bottom of which are four coats-of-arms and two figural compositions. The lid is decorated with patterns of armor, crowns and rosettes. The two scenes, carved in relief, are the *Triumph of Wladislaus IV at Panovtse* (the battle in which he defeated Abbas, Basha of Vidin, in 1633) and the *Capitulation of Sheyn at Smolensk* (a battle fought in 1634). In the latter, Wladislaus IV, mounted and in armor, and attended by Hetman Krzysztof Radziwill and knights, receives the homage of the vanquished army whose envoys make obeisance before the king on fallen standards. The restraint of the shell- and scrollwork motifs used to decorate the casket and the flat composition—seemingly without any sense of perspective—of the figures in the scenes accord with the current in early Baroque Polish art known as the Vasa style. The author of the casket was Jan Chrystian Bierpfaff, who held the title of royal goldsmith and signed his work with the initials I.C.B.

PIETER VAN DER RENNEN.
Sarcophagus of St. Stanislaus.   *pp. 92–93*

The sarcophagus now to be seen is the fourth placed on the altar of the free-standing confession—or shrine with the relics of a saint—erected in the center of Wawel Cathedral in the form of a domed *baldacchino* supported on Corinthian pillars with attached columns. The confession was built in 1626–29 on the order of Marcin Szyszkowski, Bishop of Cracow, and designed by a royal architect from Italy, Giovanni Trevano. The three earlier sarcophagi were royal gifts. The donor of the first was probably the Blessed

JAN CHRYSTIAN BIERPFAFF
17th-century royal goldsmith of Torun
The Capitulation of Sheyn at Smolensk in 1634
c. 1648
Detail of King Wladislaus IV Vasa's
burial casket.
Gilded copper.
Dimensions of casket, 226 x 107 x 105 cm;
dimensions of panel, 43 x 65 cm.
Wawel Cathedral, Cracow.

Kinga, and that of the second, Queen Jadwiga; the third, made in Augsburg in 1633 for King Sigismund III Vasa, was carried off by the Swedes in the mid-17th century. The fourth was endowed by Piotr Gembicki, Bishop of Cracow, under the terms of his will, and part of the silver sarcophagus donated by Queen Jadwiga in the 14th century was used in its construction.

An outstanding masterpiece of the goldsmith's art in Baroque Gdansk, it rests on the shoulders of four kneeling angels. The sides are divided by column-figures or praying cherubs, between which are twelve scenes from the life and miracles of St. Stanislaus. On top, two other winged cherubs kneel on the lid, supporting a bishop's pastoral staff, processional cross and mitre. The scenes between the column-figures are executed in relief with a degree of projection running from so low as to border on engraving to so high as to be almost sculpture in the round. In this way pictorial episodes have been created of such painterly value that they rank among the greatest achievements of the goldsmith's art in Baroque Europe. The sarcophagus was executed in Gdansk for the chapter of Cracow Cathedral by Piotr van der Rennen, one of the most brilliant goldsmiths working in Poland in the 17th century. The custom of making caskets in the form of sarcophagi to hold relics originated in the Middle Ages and that of St. Stanislaus endowed by Queen Jadwiga was of this kind. Its Baroque successor links back in concept to the medieval models, but is nevertheless an innovating work in European art since—together with the casket of St. Adalbert in Gniezno, also by van der Rennen—it ushered in a whole series of casket-shaped reliquaries in the Baroque style.

PIETER VAN DER RENNEN
17th-century goldsmith of Gdansk
Sarcophagus of St. Stanislaus, 1669–71
Silver, chased. 101 x 217 x 86 cm.
Wawel Cathedral, Cracow.

RADZIWILL WORKSHOPS IN NIESWIEZ. *Review of the Troops at Zabludow.*

In the 18th century the production of tapestries was started on the estates of the Radziwills, one of the most powerful noble families in Poland. The first workshop was founded by Anna Radziwill in the 1730s in Biala Podlaska, and then moved to Mira. In 1752, after her death, her son Prince Michal Kazimierz had another workshop—probably at Nieswiez, but possibly at Koreliczki—both Radziwill estates—which wove a series of tapestries with representations glorifying the Radziwill line. They were to be hung in the family seat at Nieswiez. The cartoons were executed in oil on canvas by Ksawery Dominik Heske, a painter employed at the Radziwill court who died in 1764. His designs were based on paintings, drawings and engravings by other artists which he turned into pictorial designs of an entrancing naiveté.

The weavers were mainly peasant women living on the Radziwill estates whose long years of employment in these workshops gave them a mastery of their craft. Two of them are known by name: Anastazja Markiewicz, a gardener's wife; and Maria Kulakowska, whose initials MK appear on a tapestry representing the Battle of the Slavechno River, which was less a military engagement than the suppression of a peasant revolt on the estates of the chapter of Vilnius Cathedral by the private army of Prince Michal Kazimierz Radziwill, Grand Hetman of Lithuania.

94   The tapestry with the *Review of the Troops at Zabludow,* the biggest and

RADZIWILL WORKSHOPS IN NIESWIEZ
2nd half 18th century
Review of the Troops at Zabludow
Wool tapestry; 329 x 349 cm.
National Museum, Cracow.

best preserved of the four surviving ones of a planned series of at least eight, bears the signature of Anastazja Markiewicz, the cartoon being the work of Heske who doubtless modeled it on an engraving. The scene shows Lithuanian troops being reviewed in the Byelorussian locality of Zabludow by King Augustus III (1733–63). At their head rides Michal Kazimierz Radziwill who is represented twice, once in the foreground, on a rearing horse, and again in the background at the head of squadrons of cavalry reduced to the role of *staffage*. The placing of the magnified figure of the Hetman in the center of the composition results in the picture being in effect, despite its title, an equestrian portrait of the prince.

The simplified modeling of the figure, the now faded but originally garish color, and the awkward flattened treatment of background are signs that the weavers were less than complete masters of this demanding art. On the other hand, the homespun quality of the artistic form, with its simplifications and provincial naiveté, is in keeping with the Sarmatian style in Polish art during the Baroque period.

KONSTANTY ALEKSANDROWICZ
Active 2nd half 18th century
Portrait of Karol Stanislaw Radziwill, 1786
Oil on canvas; 81.5 x 64.5 cm.
National Museum, Cracow.

KONSTANTY ALEKSANDROWICZ. *Portrait of Karol Stanislaw Radziwill.*

All the paintings known to be the work of Aleksandrowicz come from the years 1777–94 and consist mainly of portraits, or copies of portraits of the lesser and higher nobility from the former eastern borderlands of the Commonwealth. In them he achieved a skillful synthesis of the old-Polish type of portraiture known as Sarmatian, distinguished by forthright characterization of the sitter, flat treatment of figures dressed in bright hues and a wealth of meticulously rendered minutiae, with the superficial features of late Baroque European art, a knowledge of which he could have acquired in Poland from the prolific work of Marcello Bacciarelli, an Italian painter at the court of the last king of Poland, Stanislaus Augustus Poniatowski. Karol Stanislaw Radziwill (1734–90) was the owner of huge estates, which included sixteen towns and 583 villages. He was a typical product of the obscurantism prevalent among the higher nobility, which placed private interests above the public good and refused to yield up any of its anachronistic privileges, even though only reform could avert the threat of collapse that hung over Poland.

Radziwill is shown in the uniform of a general of the Lithuanian army with the Polish orders of the White Eagle and St. Stanislaus and the Russian Order of St. Andrew. The self-importance of the pose, the gaudy color, the minuteness of the details of the dress and the attempt to achieve a three-dimensional impression of the fleshy face by means of chiaroscuro make

JEAN-PIERRE NORBLIN DE LA GOURDAINE. *Breakfast in the Park at Powazki.* *p. 96*

Norblin studied at the Académie de Peinture et Sculpture in Paris under the battle-painter Francesco Casanova, at the Académie Royale and the École Royale des Élèves Protégés. From 1774 to 1804 he was painter to the court of the Czartoryski family, first at Pulawy, the family seat, then moving to Warsaw c. 1790. In the early phase of his stay in Poland he painted idyllic

MICHAL STACHOWICZ
Cracow 1768—Cracow 1825
Kosciuszko Taking the Oath in Cracow Market Square, c. 1816
Oil on canvas; 120 x 79 cm.
National Museum, Cracow.

Facing page
JEAN-PIERRE NORBLIN DE
LA GOURDAINE
Misy-Fault-Yonne, Champagne 1745—Paris 1830
Breakfast in the Park at Powazki, 1785
Decorative paneling for palace of Izabela
Czartoryska at Pulawy, near Warsaw.
Oil on canvas; 220 x 126 cm.
Czartoryski Collection,
National Museum, Cracow.

scenes in the manner of Watteau's *fêtes galantes*. In Warsaw, which was then gripped by a mood of patriotic frenzy and animated debate over democratic political reform, he began to depict in a realistic mode the social and political life of the capital and—chiefly in engravings and drawings—aspects of the Polish *moeurs* which he found so exotic and picturesque. A great many future Polish artists were trained in his studio. The *Breakfast in the Park at Powazki* was painted by Norblin in 1785 as decorative paneling for the country house of Princess Izabela Czartoryska outside Warsaw. In style it is akin to the rococo strain in French pastoral art.

MICHAL STACHOWICZ. *Kosciuszko Taking the Oath in Cracow Market Square.*

The work of Stachowicz—provincial and delightfully naive—illustrates how hard it was for Cracovian painting in the late 18th century to release

97

itself from the vice of the antiquated guild organization hobbling any kind of revitalizing in art. Stachowicz, who had received his art education in the Cracow painters guild and remained a member, painted the scene of *Kosciuszko Taking the Oath*. The painting, artlessly designed, depicts the event in the city's central square on 24 March 1794 when General Tadeusz Kosciuszko (1746–1817) pledged loyalty to the ideals of the first national insurrection and to the liberation of Poland from the rule of the three powers which had overrun and partitioned the country. The proclamations issued by Kosciuszko, who took command of the rebel army, broke new ground by recognizing the Polish peasants as full citizens and exhorting them to join actively in the struggle. His courage and exploits (he was also a hero of the American War of Independence) made him a legendary figure around whom there grew up an intense national cult.

JAN HRUZIK. *View of Kazimierz and Cracow from the South.*
Hruzik, the son of a Czech official in the Austrian public service, studied painting in Vienna and traveled in Italy, but spent most of his life in Cracow. His work consisted mainly of portraits, portrait miniatures and landscapes. The *View of Kazimierz and Cracow from the South* shows the city from the southern suburb of Krzemionki, with the low buildings of the Podgorze quarter in the foreground. The townscape is drawn with all the attention to detail of a miniaturist, though it also has some of the gracefulness of the idyllic landscapes of the Viennese late Biedermeier "Little Masters." The vista reveals the Wawel Hill complex thrusting into the horizon in the distance, possessing an established, historic configuration, the development of which began with the Instrument of Foundation in 1257 and continued until roughly the middle of the 18th century, when the last of the edifices of architectural interest visible here came into being. Immediately across the Vistula River is Kazimierz founded as a town in the 14th century by King Casimir the Great (1333–70) in the hope of making Cracow more amenable to the royal will, but which never amounted to more than a satellite. The skyline of Kazimierz is dominated by the churches of St. Catherine (the spireless one in front of Wawel Hill) and Corpus Christi to the right. To the left of Wawel Hill, on the bank of the Vistula, stands the twin-spired Church on the Rock, and across the river, further left, can be seen, on a height dedicated to the Blessed Bronislawa, Kosciuszko Mound, the monument erected in 1820–23 to the leader of the first national uprising, General Tadeusz Kosciuszko.

JAN HRUZIK
Cracow 1809—Lvov 1891
View of Kazimierz and Cracow from the South, 1849
Oil on canvas; 40 x 53 cm.
City of Cracow History Museum.

SATURNIN SWIERZNYSKI. *Interior of the Church of Our Lady in Cracow.*
After studying painting under Wojciech Korneli Stattler, at the School of Fine Arts in Cracow, Swierznyski worked as a librarian, keeper of the well-known art collection of Piotr Moszynski and teacher of drawing at St. Hyacinth's, one of the city's lycées. Throughout his life his paintings were chiefly devoted to views of Cracow, especially its historic architecture. The *Interior of the Church of Our Lady in Cracow* displays all his strengths as an artist: precise draughtsmanship with a sound grasp of perspective, color subordinated to graphic values, and accuracy of detail. It shows the church prior to the alterations made in the 19th century when the late-Baroque architectural decoration of the interior was removed and the original Gothic

forms restored. The predilection of 19th-century artists for painting the historic architecture of Cracow coincided with the rise of a more scientific kind of connoisseurship of its antiquities, which led in the latter half of the century to a development of this field of study which made the city Poland's leading center of art conservation.

PIOTR MICHALOWSKI. *The Charge at Somosierra.* p. 100
Between 1815 and 1823 Piotr Michalowski attended universities in Cracow and Göttingen, where he studied science and, among the humanities, law, English and the history of music. So thorough and versatile an education combined with natural ability opened the way to a successful career in the economic and public administration of the Kingdom of Poland, the rump state set up at the Congress of Vienna. Like many contemporary Poles, his political views were strongly affected by the fond illusions of the Napoleonic epic which had conjured up dreams of the recovery of independence. Almost as a sideline Michalowski became the most eminent pictorial artist of the Romantic period in Poland, beginning his art education in Cracow and continuing in Charlet's studio in Paris in 1832–35, where his studies also included the old masters. Among contemporary artists he particularly admired Géricault. He was a skillful painter of horses, battle-pieces and por-

PIOTR MICHALOWSKI
Hetman Stefan Czarniecki on Horseback, c. 1846
Oil on canvas, 676.5 x 59.5 cm.
National Museum, Cracow.

Facing page
PIOTR MICHALOWSKI
Cracow 100—Krzyztoporzyce, near Cracow 1855
The Charge at Somosierra, c. 1837 or 1845–55
Oil on canvas; 106 x 71 cm.
National Museum, Cracow.

traits, especially of the common people whom, for the first time in Polish art, he represented with a psychological truth shorn of all the embellishments of Romantic sentimentalism.

The *Charge at Somosierra* is an impression on the theme of a famous engagement fought in the mountains of Guadarama on 30 November 1808 by the Polish 3rd Squadron of Light Cavalry attached to the Napoleonic army during the Spanish campaign. The picture lacks any kind of topographical accuracy (to which the artist did not, for that matter, aspire), and the battle is set in a narrow ravine between steep cliffs. In Michalowski's own Romantically colored phase he aimed for an effect of lightning piercing the canvas. Dramatic tension is achieved through a composition of a bravura remarkable for the time, and through an equally impetuous, though sure, application of color.

101

PIOTR MICHALOWSKI. *Hetman Stefan Czarniecki on Horseback.*   *p. 101*

In 1796 Wawel Hill, together with the royal residence and cathedral, was taken over by the Austrian army which adapted the buildings to its own uses, damaging them in the process. But as early as the first half of the 19th century, thought was being given in Cracow to the restoration of Wawel to a splendor befitting a former seat of kings. The equestrian painting of Stefan Czarniecki (1599–1665), Field Marshal (Hetman) of the Crown, a hero of the wars with Sweden, is a sketch by Michalowski for one of a series of portraits of famous Polish generals which was to hang in Wawel Castle. The brilliant guerrilla strategist is represented seated on a rearing white stallion. The subdued color in a mellow range of warm greys, and the dense texture of the paint applied with brush-strokes of great panache, make this picture, despite its small scale, one of the masterpieces of 19th-century Polish painting.

JAN MATEJKO. *The Prussian Homage*, detail.   *pp. 103–4*

Matejko was the outstanding Polish painter of historical scenes. Apart from brief interludes devoted to studies at the academies in Munich (1859, under Hermann Anschütz) and Vienna (1860, under Christian Ruben) and exploring the art treasures of Paris, Vienna, Budapest, Prague, Constantinople and the cities of Italy (Rome, Florence, Venice, Naples), he spent most of his life in Cracow where he attended the School of Fine Arts in 1852–58, becoming its principal in 1873. He was also a fellow of the Cracow Learned Society (elected in 1864) and of many similar European bodies and academies of art. In the second half of the 19th century there was a great flowering of historical scholarship at Cracow's Jagiellonian University and this—together with the patriotic atmosphere reigning in the former capital of Poland which then formed part of the relatively liberal Austrian partition zone—molded Matejko's outlook on the national past. He was for the most part concerned with this subject matter, and what is to be admired in his work is the way in which he tried to strike a balance between the discreditable episodes in the annals of the nation and its moments of glory. He hoped that his pictorial history of Poland would help to awaken a sense of national identity.

The Prussian Homage was painted in 1882 when Matejko was forty-four years of age and at the height of his powers. It depicts the ceremony on 10 April 1525 when Albert Hohenzollern, the last Grand Master of the Teutonic Knights of the Cross and the first secular Duke of Prussia, publicly acknowledged in the central square of Cracow the overlordship of the King of Poland in the person of Sigismund I of the Jagiellonian dynasty. The focus of both the theme and the composition of the picture is the representation of the king in majesty and Hohenzollern kneeling before him in homage. Around them in this solemn, yet dramatic scene stands a crowd of supporting witnesses, some of whom have been given the features of prominent figures in the contemporary Cracow world of learning and the arts. In Bartolommeo Berrecci, the Italian architect who worked at the court of Sigismund I in the 16th century, we can see a self-portrait of Matejko himself. Through the sumptuous pageantry of the occasion and the grave and stately

102

Pp. 103, 104
JAN MATEJKO
Cracow 1838—Cracow 1893
The Prussian Homage, 1882, details
Oil on canvas; 388 x 785 cm.
National Museum, Cracow.

demeanor of the participants Matejko conveyed the emotions evoked in him by the Golden Age of Polish culture which came in the 16th century under the reigns of the last rulers of the house of Jagiello. The style of the painting reflects a profound enchantment with the Venetian masters of the late Cinquecento and with Rubens, whose influences were creatively transmuted in a manner befitting the great talent of a 19th-century artist who looked to history for the inspiration of the form as well as the theme of his works.

Prior to Matejko, the depiction of scenes from national history had been undertaken by artists of varying ability; but he raised this genre to heights which matched the loftiness of the Polish Romantic poets. Matejko's vision of the past was too overpowering to be sustained by his pupils and imitators. Although the most gifted of them, such as Jacek Malczewski, Stanislaw Wyspianski and Jozef Mehoffer, did not abstain from subjects of a similarly national character, they treated them along wholly different lines.

JAN MATEJKO. *The Astronomer Mikolaj Kopernik*, or
Conversation with God.   *p. 106*

The great astronomer Nicolaus Copernicus (Mikolaj Kopernik), the pride of Polish learning in the 16th century and the discoverer of heliocentricism, attended Jagiellonian University in Cracow in 1491–95, a time when Renaissance humanism was in full flower in the city. There, too, his revolutionary theory immediately aroused ardent support, and in subsequent centuries his life and work continued to be an object of undying interest and veneration. The approach of the quatercentenary of his birth in 1873 acted as an impetus to intensified study of his legacy and to the organization of anniversary celebrations. Matejko's contribution to the jubilee took the form of two paintings: a large canvas he entitled *The Astronomer Mikolaj Kopernik*, or *Conversation with God* which adorns the main hall of the University, and this smaller sketch conceived as a model for the finished picture. Both depict the astronomer seated on the terrace of his observatory in Frombork against a dark blue sky with the cathedral in the background. Attitude and gesture make it graphically clear that he has been portrayed at the moment of revelation or the truth of his discovery. Around him are scattered astronomical instruments.

JAN MATEJKO. *John III Sobieski Presenting Canon Denhoff With*
a Letter to the Pope Reporting the Victory over the Turks
at Vienna in 1683.   *pp. 108–109*

The victory over the Turks in the siege of Vienna in 1683 was largely due to the Polish forces under the command of King John III Sobieski. The bicentenary of this victory inspired Matejko to paint two pictures. One, a huge canvas entitled *Sobieski at Vienna* and begun in 1879, was donated by him to Pope Leo XIII in 1883 and may now be admired in the Vatican. The other, much smaller, is sufficiently different to be considered an independent work, which, in view of its sketch-like nature, offers a closer insight into the technique of the greatest Polish 19th-century exponent of history painting. Matejko's oil sketches are vivid demonstrations of the expressively visionary quality of his work, embodied in a dynamic management of composition and painterly values exemplified in the richly diversified and luminous texture of this canvas.

P. 106
JAN MATEJKO
The Astronomer Mikolaj Kopernik or
Conversation with God, 1871
Oil on canvas; 41.5 x 52.5 cm.
National Museum, Cracow.

Pp. 108–109
JAN MATEJKO
John II Sobieski Presenting Canon Denhoff
with a Letter to the Pope Reporting the
Victory over the Turks at Vienna, 1880
Oil on canvas; 58 x 100 cm.
National Museum, Cracow.

MAURYCY GOTTLIEB. *Ahasuerus.*   *p. 110*

Gottlieb began his art education in Lvov and then continued his studies in Vienna (under Karl Mayer and Karl Blaas), history painting (under Karl Wurzinger and Heinrich von Angeli), in Munich (under Karl Piloty), and in Cracow where he arrived, at the prompting of Jan Matejko, in 1879, and died shortly afterward at the age of twenty-three. The chief subjects of his paintings were Jewish themes and portraits. The title of this picture refers to the Jew of medieval legend who was condemned to wander over the earth until the Second Coming for refusing to help Christ on the way to Golgotha. The face of this eternal vagabond is a self-portrait of Gottlieb which demonstrates all the qualities of a talent cut off in its prime: a subtle harmony of colors emphasized by scumbled pigments and evoking associations with Rembrandt, meticulous composition and precision of draughtsmanship employed to construct pictures of great emotional power.

HENRYK SIEMIRADZKI. *The Torches of Nero.*   *p. 111*

After receiving a degree in natural sciences at the University of Kharkov in the Ukraine, Siemiradzki entered the Academy of Fine Arts in Petersburg and then studied in Munich under Piloty before finally settling in Rome where his work consisted chiefly of scenes from the life and history of the ancient world. Despite the barrier of distance, he remained in close touch with events and people in his native Poland. The subject of *The Torches of Nero,* also known as *The Candlesticks of Christianity,* was taken from Tacitus' account (*Annales,* Book XV, 44) of the Roman emperor, Lucius Domitius Nero's accusation of the Christians of being responsible for the fire of Rome in A.D. 64 and ordering them to be put to death by burning at the stake in the gardens of the imperial palace.

The theme dwells on the tragic moment when the bonfires are lit under the bound Christians in the presence of the Emperor surrounded by a throng of courtiers, and the huge canvas was awarded a gold medal of honor at the Paris Salon of 1878. The attention to detail and the theatrical attitudes of the onlookers, too worldly to feign more than a passing interest in the harrowing spectacle, belong to the stock-in-trade of the Naturalist school of academic painting in Europe of which Siemiradzki was an eminent representative. The anecdotal means of expression, the insistence on the classical rules of unity of time, place and action, and the element of pretentious ceremony in the composition are typical of the kind of painting designed to gratify the tastes of the middle and wealthy classes that arose in the second half of the 19th century. *The Torches of Nero* was donated by the artist to the city of Cracow in 1879 to launch the collections of Poland's first national museum which was to be opened that year in the old Cloth Hall on Market Square.

TADEUSZ AJDUKIEWICZ. *Portrait of Helena Modrzejewska.* *p. 112*

Ajdukiewicz studied at the School of Fine Arts in Cracow and then in Munich under Josef Brandt, Otto Seitz and Alexander Wagner. He later traveled in France, Egypt and the Middle East. His elegant portraits and his

MAURYCY GOTTLIEB
Drohobycz 1856—Cracow 1879
Ahasuerus, 1876
Oil on canvas; 63 x 53 cm.
National Museum, Cracow.

battle pieces brought him to the attention of the imperial court, which resulted in his going to Vienna where, at the emperor's behest, he was given the use of Hans Makart's studio upon the latter's death in 1884.

The portrait of Helena Modrzejewska (1840–1909) was painted in Warsaw prior to Ajdukiewicz's departure for Vienna. It represents the greatest of Polish actresses, who became world-famous under the more pronounceable name of Modjeska. In 1876, having made a name in Poland, she crossed the Atlantic, established herself on the American stage and toured Europe frequently, also visiting her native country. Her performances in Shakespeare became legendary. The notable feature of the portrait, which follows the formal convention typical of the official court art of the second half of the 19th century, is the artist's concern with elegance of pose, stateliness of costume and richness of secondary detail calculated to enhance the glamor of the sitter. These external trappings are painted with all the surface skills of the Naturalist school, a point that was much appreciated at the time.

WLADYSLAW PODKOWINSKI. *Frenzy.* *p. 113*

Podkowinski was one of the Polish artists (another of note was Jozef Pankiewicz) who introduced to Poland in a rather superficial manner the principles of Impressionist painting from France, especially Monet, with whose

HENRYK SIEMIRADZKI
Byelgorod, near Kharkov 1834—Strzalkowo, near Czestochowa 1902
The Torches of Nero, 1876, detail
Oil on canvas; 385 x 704 cm.
National Museum, Cracow.

work he had become acquainted in 1889, on his first visit to Paris, which lasted only nine months. Toward the end of his life, in failing health and shattered by an unhappy love affair, he created this enormous canvas which he then, in a fit of passion, tried to destroy. It was painted at a time when, after his short-lived fascination with Impressionism, he turned to somber, symbolical pictures with almost monochromatic color schemes in which blacks and whites predominated. Because of its startling composition and decidedly erotic tinge, *Frenzy* is a very popular work in Poland, although it has occasionally come in for attacks by fanatical guardians of morality who have denounced it as an affront to decency and been cited by art critics as a textbook example of near-kitsch.

WLADYSLAW PODKOWINSKI
Warsaw 1866—Warsaw 1896
Frenzy, 1894
Oil on canvas; 310 x 275 cm.
National Museum, Cracow.

JOZEF BRANDT. *Encounter on a Bridge.* p. 114

The final direction taken by the painting of Jozef Brandt emerged from his introduction in Paris to Juliusz Kossak—who had been much impressed by his early work—and a journey they made together to the Ukraine and Podolia. In 1862–66 Brandt studied at the Munich Academy (under Franz Adam, Piloty and Theodor Horschelt) and before long his studio became the meeting place of that city's colony of Polish painters. Once a year he traveled to the Ukraine, Podolia and Volhynia, while at the Bavarian court he was a popular figure honored with numerous awards and distinctions. The chief subjects of his pictures were scenes, painted with enormous vigor, of military encounters and army life in the old eastern borderlands of the Commonwealth during the 17th-century wars with the Cossacks, Tatars and Turks. They are a pictorial counterpart of Henryk Sienkiewicz's romantic legends of the Polish gentry's struggles with the enemies marauding at large in the boundless steppes of the Ukraine, or the Swedes invading from overseas in the mid-17th century. In the *Encounter on a Bridge*, which shows a hurtling equipage forcing a wood-distiller's cart into a ditch, can be seen all the characteristics of Brandt's mature style: bravura composition and ebullient brushwork. The sureness and virtuosity which he brought to the copying of nature, especially in the depiction of horses, mark him as one of the foremost exponents of Polish Naturalism.

STANISLAW WITKIEWICZ. *Foehn.* p. 114

Witkiewicz was primarily an art critic of a Positivist persuasion and a spirited opponent of esthetic idealism. Advocating a realistic style of painting true to nature, shorn of all philosophical, literary or narrative undertones, he believed analysis of form to be the proper yardstick of a work's worth. Of lesser caliber as a painter, he studied at Petersburg and Munich and then settled in the mountain village of Zakopane where he proceeded to seek a revival of the highland style of architecture and decoration, which had been swamped by pseudo-Alpine imitations. An ardent champion of the work of Aleksander and Maksymilian Gierymaki and Jozef Chelmonski—outstanding representatives of the Realistic school in Polish art of the late 19th century—he tended in his own painting to succumb to their influence. *Foehn* has something of the haunting quality of the nocturnes of the Munich school, and makes its impact precisely through an analogous evocation of nightfall and storm clouds swirling over the Tatra Mountains.

Facing page
TADEUSZ AJDUKIEWICZ
Wieliczka 1852—Cracow 1916
Portrait of Helena Modrzejewska, 1880
Oil on canvas; 262 x 146 cm.
National Museum, Cracow.

JOZEF CHELMONSKI. *Storm.*   *p. 115*

Chelmonski began his art education in Warsaw and continued it at the Munich Academy (under Strähuber and Anschütz) where he came into contact with the local Polish artists' colony. From 1875 to 1887 he lived in Paris, where he enjoyed a considerable vogue and received many awards. At the height of his success (many of his pictures were sold in England and the United States by the Parisian art dealer Goupil) he left Paris and settled in Warsaw before eventually returning to his estate at Kuklowka in Mazovia, central Poland.

JOZEF BRANDT
Szczebrzeszyn 1841—Radom 1915
Encounter on a Bridge, 1888
Oil on canvas; 100 x 200 cm.
National Museum, Cracow.

STANISLAW WITKIEWICZ
Poszawsze, Samogitia 1850—Lovran 1915
Foehn, 1895
Oil on canvas, 93 x 142 cm.
National Museum, Cracow.

Storm, painted in 1896, pinpoints the strengths of his realistic style in capturing the moods of the scenery in the Mazovian plain. No Polish painter equaled Chelmonski's ability to blend the characteristic topography of the Polish lowlands with emotionally charged depictions of the life of the common people. His sense of the close relationship between nature and rustic existence had echoes in the contemporary writing and thinking of the Polish intelligensia which tended, not without overtones of mysticism, to see the peasant as the personification of the eternal forces of nature. These paintings, usually restricted in color range but making up for this by rich variations of tone, scarcely underwent any significant development save for a superficial bow to Impressionism, remaining firmly outside the mainstream of change in Polish art brought by Symbolism and Modernism.

ALEKSANDER GIERYMSKI. *The Feast of Trumpets.* *p. 116*
Gierymski completed his art studies in 1868–73 at the Academy in Munich (where his teachers were Strähuber, Anschütz and Piloty). From 1873 to 1879 he lived in Rome, spent the next eight years in Warsaw and another three in Munich, and then moved to Paris where he remained until 1893. From 1895 until his death in 1901, apart from a two-year stay in Cracow, he worked abroad. He was an outstanding Polish practitioner of realism whose language he tried—in a manner independent of the accomplishments of the French Impressionists—to synthesize with experimentation in color and light.
The composition shows Jews praying beside the Vistula River in Warsaw during the Yom Kippur holiday on the tenth day of the Jewish New Year, the end of which is announced by the blowing of trumpets. The twilight mood is captured in masterly fashion, a sense of the dying day reflected in the calm waters of the broad river being achieved by means of glistening texture and astonishing harmony of color. The picture, which is one of three versions of this theme essayed by Gierymski, ranks among the outstanding works of Polish 19th-century painting.

STANISLAW WYSPIANSKI. *Polonia.* *p. 117*
A man of versatile talents, Wyspianski was, among other things, the leading master of the visual arts in the Young Poland modernist movement. A

JOZEF CHELMONSKI
Boczki, near Lowicz 1849—Kublowka, Mazovia, 1914
Storm, 1896
Oil on canvas; 107 x 163 cm.
National Museum, Cracow.

graduate of Jagiellonian University (political history, art history and literature) and the School of Fine Arts in Cracow (where one of his teachers was Jan Matejko), he traveled widely in Europe. In Paris he came into contact with the Nabis and Gauguin. He was a painter (working chiefly in pastels), poet, brilliant dramatist and theater reformer. He also designed interiors, stained glass and books, his work in this last field giving birth to some of the finest achievements of the printer's art at the turn of the century.

Brought up in a patriotic atmosphere, smarting under the humiliating defeats suffered by generations of Poles in their struggle to regain freedom, raised on the Polish Romantic literature which had made the issue of liberty one of its central concerns, and conversant with the legendary optimism in the later work of his teacher, Jan Matejko, he put forward new and often bitter answers of his own to these Polish moral and philosophical heartsearchings. They were articulated chiefly in his plays, but in his monumental designs for stained-glass windows for the cathedrals of Cracow and Lvov we can also find forceful expressions of his view of history and national legends.

Part of the cartoon he made for the Lvov Cathedral window, *Polonia* punc-

STANISLAW WYSPIANSKI
Self-portrait of the Artist with Wife, 1904
Pastel on cardboard; 47.5 x 62.2 cm.
National Museum, Cracow.

tures the myth of heroic Poland with its representation of a swooning figure, the sword fallen from her grasp and no longer capable of stirring
anyone to action. The symbolic message is heightened by supplicants with
arms raised in the upper right corner of the picture, and a twisted rosebush
with jagged thorns in the lower left corner.

STANISLAW WYSPIANSKI. *Self-Portrait with Wife.*
Wyspianski's self-portrait with his wife, Teodora Teofila, a peasant girl
from the village of Zabno near Tarnow, possesses all the characteristics of
his mature portrait work: simplicity of composition, a pliant *Art Nouveau*
line, flat areas of purely applied color, and a certain hint of melancholy in
the face of the artist. The frequency with which the intellectuals of Young
Poland, themselves of middle-class background, married into the peasantry
was not just a matter of a passing whim or vogue, but also sprang from reasons rooted in the broader phenomenon of a belief in social solidarity. A
literary commentary, tinged with subtle irony, on this fascination with the
bucolic was provided by Wyspianski himself in his dramatic masterpiece
Wesele (The Wedding) written in 1901, prompted by the real-life wedding
of his poet friend, Lucjan Rydel, to a peasant girl from the village of
Bronowice outside Cracow.

STANISLAW WYSPIANSKI. *Rudawa Landscape.*   *p. 119*
Throughout his life Wyspianski was a keen observer of nature, and the
studies of flora in the Cracow region collected in his "herbaria" form a

large part of his legacy of drawings. In his landscape painting a number of ways of viewing nature can be distinguished. The early approach came close to an idiosyncratic Impressionism, the best known cycle being his pastels of Kosciuszko Mound in Cracow which are reminiscent, in their repeated re-working of the theme, of Monet's landscape sets, but whose formal values also suggest a fascination with the atmosphere of Hokusai's *36 Views of Mount Fuji*. The riverside flats painted with broad individual strokes and the twisted jumble of shrubbery in the foreground make the *Rudawa Land-scape* a picture of considerable power, but one which also has the haunting air of melancholy that emanates from the whole of Wyspianski's work.

JOZEF MEHOFFER. *Portrait of the Artist's Wife.* p. 120

Mehoffer attended the School of Fine Arts in Cracow (where one of his teachers was Matejko) and then studied in Paris (Académie Julian, École des Arts Décoratifs, Académie Colarossi and École Nationale des Beaux-Arts). In 1895 he won the first prize at an international competition for stained-glass windows for the Church of St. Nicholas in Fribourg, Switzerland. The execution of this project, his magnum opus in every sense (over 200 designs, some of them almost thirteen meters high), occupied him until 1934. He was one of the founders of the "Sztuka" Society of Polish Artists, and a member of the Vienna Secession and the Société Nationale des Beaux-Arts in Paris. In 1902 he joined the faculty of the Academy of Fine Arts in Cracow. His works were frequently awarded prizes at international exhibitions. Next to Wyspianski, he was the foremost exponent of Polish Modernism. In his mural paintings he came under the influence of the decorative strain in *Art Nouveau.* His canvases frequently veer toward Symbolism. He was also an accomplished portraitist.

A favorite subject was his wife whom he painted in stylish costumes and matching interiors filled with decorative objects. Her portraits have an entrancingly exquisite harmony of color. The one illustrated here shows a

STANISLAW WYSPIANSKI
Rudawa Landscape, 1905
Pastel on cardboard; 45 x 63.5 cm.
National Museum, Cracow.

JOZEF MEHOFFER
Ropczyce, Little Poland, 1868—Wadowice,
near Cracow, 1946
Portrait of the Artist's Wife, 1904
Oil on canvas; 147 x 80 cm.
National Museum, Cracow.

woman standing in a brightly lit room lost in thought, a twig of pine dangling from her hand. Her somber, abstracted air contrasts oddly with the furnishings of the room—harmonium, easy chair, toys—which suggest the carefree atmosphere of a holiday resort.

JACEK MALCZEWSKI. *The Unknown Note.* p. 121

Malczewski studied painting at the School of Fine Arts in Cracow (one of his teachers being Matejko) and at the École des Beaux-Arts in Paris (under Heinrich Lehmann). He traveled in Italy, and in 1884–5 visited the Middle East, making drawings for an archaeological expedition organized by Count Lanckoronski. He taught at the Academy of Fine Arts in Cracow (serving as its Rector), and was one of the founders of the "Sztuka" Society of Polish Artists. Enamored of Polish Romantic poetry, especially Juliusz Slowacki, he developed themes drawn from the martyrology of the nation following the defeat of the January Insurrection (1863). Painted in an almost monochromatic color range with a multiplicity of symbolic meanings, they were inspired by Polish history, the Bible and mythology, and delineated with incredible precision, often with color schemes alternating between strident discords and captivating harmony. His iconography testifies to a stupendous imagination, weaving together different motifs into a whole of highly ambiguous content. The sources of his symbolic art lie in the romantically dramatic course of Polish destiny, in which an exceptional role was assigned to the artist.

In *The Unknown Note*, a portrait of one of Malczewski's friends, Stanislaw Bryniarski—another Cracow painter—we see the latter bemusedly listening to the music of a Faun—"unknown" because it is lost on ordinary ears. The richness of Malczewski's imagination and the metaphorical power of his art make him a distinguished representative of European as well as Polish Modernism and Symbolism.

WLADYSLAW SLEWINSKI. *Study of a Woman Combing Her Hair.* p. 122

From 1888 onward Slewinski lived in Le Pouldu, and also in Paris, where he studied at the Académie Julian and the Académie Colarossi. In 1889 he met and struck up a friendship with Gauguin, and from 1890 to 1895 he belonged to the Pont Aven group. In 1905 he returned to Poland and stayed there until 1910, chiefly in Cracow, Poronin and Warsaw, where he taught at the School of Fine Arts. In 1910 he settled for good in Doëlan, Brittany. He thought highly of the work of Gauguin, the chief distinctive feature of his own being a much more subdued color range restricted to greys, deep browns, and muted greens and blues with only an occasional counterpoint of brighter hues. The fluidity of line and sketchiness of the flat-painted interior indicate links not only with the Pont-Aven artists, but also with Japanese woodcut then being rediscovered in Europe.

OLGA BOZNANSKA. *Portrait of Gabrielle Reval.* p. 123

Cracow and then Munich were the scenes of Olga Boznanska's art education. In 1889 her awareness of what she sought in painting took her to Paris where, save for a few brief intervals, she lived until the end of her life. In 1898 she became a member of the "Sztuka" Society of Polish Artists and in

1904 of the Société Nationale des Beaux-Arts. She took part in all the Society's exhibitions between 1896 and 1926. In 1912 she was awarded the French Legion of Honor and in 1938 the Order of Polonia Restituta. She made her reputation primarily with her portraits of prominent figures in the French and Polish worlds of art and culture, developing an individual style that fused a very personal interpretation of the achievements of Impressionism and a fascination with the work of Goya and Velázquez. A juxtaposition of her study of Gabrielle Reval, a well-known French writer (1870–1938) with Goya's portrait of Maria Josephe brings out the Boznanska hallmarks. She painted her pictures on thick cardboard in a restricted color range of white, rich-toned greys, subdued blues and greens, and, in her earlier work, sharply contrasting splashes of black. This spectrum was completed by the ochres of the unpainted areas of the cardboard. The

JACEK MALCZEWSKI
Radowm 1854—Cracow 1929
The Unknown Note, 1902
Oil on canvas; 42 x 63 cm.
National Museum, Cracow.

construction of the figures out of vibrating blotches of color embedded in the rough surface of the ground and the avoidance of gleaming varnishes make the sitters appear to be wreathed in a misty glow which does not, however, blur the forcefulness of the psychological characterization.

WOJCEICH WEISS. *Demon.* *p. 124*

Weiss began his art studies in Cracow (where one of his teachers was Matejko) and continued them in Paris (1899–1900), after which he made a journey to Italy. In 1902 he became a member of the "Sztuka" Society of Polish Artists, and from 1902 onward was associated with the Academy of Fine Arts in Cracow, becoming a professor in 1910 and serving a number of terms as Rector. He took an active part in exhibitions organized in the art centers of Europe and America at which he obtained various awards and medals. His work went through a large number of phases. *Demon*, which belongs to his early period, ranks among the best achievements of Polish Modernism. The theme is clearly drawn from the bohemian life of the Latin Quarter, while the treatment owes much to the Symbolist views of Stanislaw Przybyszewski (1868–1927), a prominent figure in European Modern-

WLADYSLAW SLEWINSKI
Bialynin 1854—Paris 1918
Study of a Woman Combing Her Hair, 1897
Oil on canvas; 64 x 91 cm.
National Museum, Cracow.

122

ism and the ideologist of Polish Expressionism. The carefully contrived color range, restricted to flat splashes of black, muted yellows, subdued browns, greys and faded reds, is frequent in the early Weiss who, regardless of period, was always a highly sophisticated colorist.

WITOLD WOJTKIEWICZ. *Fantasy.* *p. 125*
Wojtkiewicz, one of the most talented artists of the Modernist period in Poland, had no systematic art education, though he studied off and on in Warsaw, Petersburg and Cracow, the city which he made his home and left only

when stricken by the disease which caused his death at the age of only thirty. It was here that he painted his expressive canvases abounding in chimerical motifs, creating a world of shadowy metaphor. He belonged to a number of groups, including the "Sztuka" Society of Polish Artists. His sole one-man show was organized for him at the Galerie Drouot in Paris in 1907 by André Gide who, together with Maurice Denis, discovered his work at an exhibition in Berlin. His pictures are peopled by old men engaged in childlike activities or children posing as aged invalids. Both occupy an eccentric world of circus and fairground or haunted palace and magic garden. In these ironic, riveting paintings, of which *Fantasy* is a good example, Wojtkiewicz tried to identify and lay bare the deeply hidden, often subconscious mechanism of human emotions.

WOJCIECH WEISS
Leorda, Romania, 1875—Cracow 1950
Demon, 1904
Oil on canvas; 65.5 x 96 cm.
National Museum, Cracow.

WITOLD WOJTKIEWICZ
Warsaw 1879—Warsaw 1909
Fantasy, 1906
Oil on canvas; 35.5 x 41 cm.
National Museum, Cracow.

LEON WYCZOLKOWSKI. *Ploughing in the Ukraine.*   *p. 126*
Wyczolkowski completed at the Munich Academy the art studies he had
begun in Warsaw under Wojciech Gerson and in Cracow under Matejko.
He himself taught at the Warsaw Academy of Fine Arts and, briefly, at the
Cracow School of Fine Arts. He was one of the organizers of the "Sztuka"
Society of Polish Artists. His short life coincided with a period of great
upheaval in Polish art, moving in his own work from history painting,
via Impressionism and Symbolism, to a very idiosyncratic variety of Post-
Impressionism. He was also an outstanding print-maker. *Ploughing in the
Ukraine* followed his second sojourn in Paris and his assimilation of the
principles of Divisionism.

WLADYSLAW PODKOWINSKI. *Wilczyce Landscape.*
This painting, also entitled *Wilczyce—Fields of Clover*, was painted at a time when Podkowinski was experimenting with French Impressionism which he had had the opportunity to study more closely in 1889. An effect

LEON WYCZOLKOWSKI
Miastkow Koscielny 1852—Warsaw 1936
Ploughing in the Ukraine, 1892
Oil on canvas, 73.5 x 121.5 cm.
National Museum, Cracow.

WLADYSLAW PODKOWINSKI
Warsaw 1866—Warsaw 1895
Wilczyce Landscape, 1893
Oil on canvas; 64 x 81 cm.
National Museum, Cracow.

of depth is achieved by means of flat areas of color, while the abandonment of the Divisionism used in other works of this vintage draws attention to qualities more typical of Post-Impressionism, a stage at which Podkowinski arrived spontaneously and by his own route.

JAN STANISLAWSKI. *Barns in Pustowarnia.*

After studying mathematics at Warsaw University, Stanislawski entered the Institute of Technology in Petersburg, but left without graduating and returned to Warsaw where he began art studies continued in Cracow and Paris. There he made a name as a landscape painter. He also traveled widely, particularly in Italy. In 1897 he was appointed professor of landscape at the Academy of Fine Arts in Cracow. He was a great advocate of outdoor sketching, and many Polish landscape painters benefited from his teaching. Most of his paintings are small.

A number of them were painted, at different periods in his life, in Pustowarnia, an estate in the Ukraine. The sweep of the brushstroke employed in the *Barns in Pustowarnia* to create the cloudy sky indicates that it is one of his later works. By then Stanislawski had developed a distinctive manner of his own in which the discoveries of Impressionism were fused with a compressed, atmospheric perception of nature. In the words of a contemporary writer and art critic, Zenon Przesmycki, editor of the journal *Chimera*, he

JAN STANISLAWSKI
Olshana, Ukraine 1860—Cracow 1907
Barns in Pustowarnia, c. 1903
Oil on cardboard; 24 x 32.5 cm.
National Museum, Cracow.

possessed the remarkable gift of "enclosing in a single detail a sense of the whole of nature."

JOZEF PANKIEWICZ. *Still-Life with Fruit and Knife.*
Pankiewicz studied in Warsaw (under Wojciech Gerson) and Petersburg. In the years between the world wars he traveled widely in Europe, with a long sojourn in France. Together with Podkowinski he introduced to Polish art a somewhat superficial version of French Impressionism. In 1925 he joined the faculty of a newly established branch of the Cracow Academy in Paris, where a number of students proceeded to form a group called the Paris Committee or Kapists (from its Polish initials KP). Pankiewicz himself traveled a path from Realism via Impressionism and Symbolism to a Post-Impressionist colorism. Through his teaching as well as his work, he exerted a strong influence on Polish Colorism before and after World War II. He remained under the spell of the art of Cézanne and Renoir, and was a friend of Bonnard.

The *Still-Life with Fruit and Knife* has obvious affinities with Cézanne. It was donated to the National Museum by Feliks Jasienski, a personal friend of the artist and one of the foremost Polish collectors of the 20th century, to

JOSEF PANKIEWICZ
Lublin 1866—Marseilles 1940
Still-Life with Fruit and Knife, 1909
Oil on canvas; 52 x 65.5 cm.
National Museum, Cracow.

whom the Museum owes its Far Eastern gallery. This latter collection, donated in 1920, is among the biggest of its kind in Poland (especially as regards the art of Japan) and also occupies a place of some note in Europe.

ZBIGNIEW PRONASZKO. *Formist Nude.*
Pronaszko began his art studies at the School of Fine Arts in Kiev and completed them (under Teodor Axentowicz) at the Academy in Cracow. He traveled to Italy, Paris, Munich and Vienna, becoming acquainted with the newest artistic currents in Europe. A sculptor and stage designer as well as painter, he was one of the founders of the Polish Formists group organized in 1917 by a number of avant-garde artists with leanings toward Cubism

ZBIGNIEW PRONASZKO
Derepczyn, near Jampola 1885—Cracow 1958
Formist Nude, 1917
Oil on canvas; 112 x 65 cm.
National Museum, Cracow.

and Expressionism.

The *Formist Nude*, painted in violet and greyish tones, comes, as the title indicates, from the "Formist" period in Pronaszko's work, with its alternating pattern of oval and angular shapes showing him experimenting in the direction of Cubism. At the time he described what he was trying to do in the following terms: "Observing an object . . . I do not see it solely from the front; on the contrary, all its various planes impress themselves upon my imagination and only by re-assembling them in the picture do I obtain its full expression, its essence."

TADEUSZ MAKOWSKI. *In the Studio.*

Makowski studied at the Cracow Academy of Fine Arts under Stanislawski and Mehoffer. In 1908 he went to Paris where he associated with artists of the Cubist school and exhibited with them in 1913. His work developed under the influence of Cubism. In France he was considered a leading colorist of the École de Paris. After his death in 1932, a group of friends, including Gromaire, formed in Paris a Society of Friends of Tadeusz Makowski.

The subjects of many of the 600-odd pictures which he painted are children who, though represented in simplified, "cubic" form, in no way forfeit an individual quality. *In the Studio*, which comes from Makowski's most fully developed period, demonstrates his concern with color values and a simplification of form which sprang not so much from the adoption of certain theoretical principles as from analytical observation of nature and the cast of his mind.

JAN CYBIS. *French Landscape.* p. 131

Cybis studied under Müller at the Academy of Fine Arts in Wroclaw (1919–21) and then in Cracow (1921–24) under Mehoffer, Pienkowski and

TADEUSZ MAKOWSKI
Oswiecim 1882—Paris 1932
In the Studio, 1930
Oil on canvas; 46 x 55 cm.
National Museum, Cracow.

Pankiewicz. He joined the Paris Committee group and remained with them in Paris until 1931. After the war he taught at the Academy of Fine Arts in Warsaw. His paintings consist chiefly of landscapes, but also include still-lifes and portraits.

The *French Landscape*, painted probably in the region of Montereau or, according to others, Moret, is a typical example of Polish Post-Impressionist colorism as practiced by the Kapists. They held that, though a picture arose out of the artist's contact with nature, it was not to be a direct imitation, but a distillation of certain theoretical assumptions in which color was the basic element. This offshoot of French Post-Impressionism gave rise in Polish art to a stream that swung away from the national concerns so characteristic of the 19th century and Modernism and concentrated on the formal problems of what the Kapists called "painterly resolution of the canvas."

This artistic philosophy was carried over into the postwar period by the survivors of the old Paris Committee, many of whom were recruited to the faculties of art schools.

STANISLAW IGNACY WITKIEWICZ. *Portrait of Professor*
Dr. Stefan Szuman.   *p. 132*

Best known as a dramatist, philosopher, art theorist and novelist, Stanislaw Ignacy Witkiewicz ("Witkacy") was taught the rudiments of art by his painter and art-critic father, Stanislaw. A member of the Polish Formists group, he traveled widely in France, Italy and Germany. His esthetics, in many respects ahead of their time, was set out in two works: *The New Forms in Painting and the Misconceptions Arising from Them* (Warsaw, 1919) and *Essays in Aesthetics* (Cracow, 1922). His avant-garde plays now form part of the canon of contemporary European drama. In his theory of Pure Form he rejected everything that was a reflection of reality, maintaining that the essence of the work of art was "constituted . . . by formal constructions which, depending on the content encompassed by them, act on the spectator or listener through the direct mediation of their constructional nature." His expressive compositions of the years 1919–24, seething with

JAN CYBIS
Wroblin, Opole Silesia 1897—Warsaw 1972
French Landscape, c. 1928
Oil on canvas; 34 x 47 cm.
National Museum, Cracow.

ARTUR NACHT-SAMBORSKI
Sambor 1898—Warsaw 1974
White Portrait, 1962
Oil on cardboard; 60 x 49 cm.
National Museum, Cracow.

STANISLAW IGNACY WITKIEWICZ
Warsaw 1885—Jeziory near Polesiu 1939
Portrait of Prof. Dr. Stefan Szuman, 1929
Pastel on cardboard; 62.7 x 46.7 cm.
National Museum, Cracow.

eerie fantasies bodied forth in "shreds and tangles," reveal the drama of an artist who put forward the theoretical basis of abstract art, but was unable to flesh it out in his paintings. This sense of frustration or, in his own phrase, "drama of Pure Form" led him to abandon serious painting around 1925 and start a commercial enterprise called the "S.I.Witkiewicz Portrait Company." This ironic gesture summed up the tragic conflict of an artist smarting under the nonfulfillment of his theoretical visions. Although the portraits, made in a mixed technique of charcoal, crayon, pencil and pastels, were not conceived as art, they are nevertheless provocative exercises in experimentation. Diversified in style, these commissions executed strictly

133

according to the firm's rulebook cannot conceal an undercurrent of obsessive, often violently disturbing dialogue with the expressive potential of artistic form. Some of these portraits were painted while under the controlled influence of drugs (a fact noted on this picture in code). Among them are works which are more or less realistic likenesses of the sitter (Type A in the firm's nomenclature) and others in which portraiture was merely a pretext for compositions bordering on the abstract. The portrait of Professor Szuman (1889–1972), a psychologist of distinguished achievement in the investigation of children's art and a personal friend, belongs in the former category.

PIOTR POTWOROWSKI
Warsaw 1898—Warsaw 1962
Oval Cornwall Landscape, 1957
Emulsion on canvas; 132 x 60 cm.
National Museum, Cracow.

ARTUR NACHT-SAMBORSKI. *White Portrait.*   p. 133

A student of Mehoffer and Weiss at the Cracow Academy of Fine Arts, Nacht-Samborski worked out the ultimate shape of his style in the course of stays in Paris, Berlin and Vienna. In Paris he became associated with the Kapists, with whom he shared an interest in Post-Impressionist tonal construction. After the war he served on the faculties of the College of Fine Arts in Sopot and the Academy of Fine Arts in Warsaw. The *White Portrait*, with its harmonized areas of color and firmly outlined, soft modeling of the figure, is a personal interpretation of the principles of Polish Colorism amplified by postwar trends in Polish and European painting. It represents one of the best achievements of the artist's later period.

PIOTR POTWOROWSKI   *Oval Cornwall Landscape.*

Potworowski studied architecture at the Warsaw Polytechnic, and painting under Konrad Krzyzanowski in Warsaw and Pankiewicz in Cracow. He was one of the organizers of the Paris Committee in 1924 and remained with the Kapists in Paris until 1933, attending activities in Léger's studio. When the Germans invaded Poland he made his way via Sweden to England where, after the war, he taught at an art school in Corsham, near Bath. He was a member of the London Group (1954) and the Royal West of England Academy (1956). In 1958 he returned to Poland and was a professor at the Colleges of Art in Poznan and Sopot. In 1960 he received a Guggenheim Award.

Because of the profound transmutation of nature and its reduction to geometric forms enclosed in an oval, his Cornish landscape can be seen as an abstract work. The constructional compactness of Potworowski's later paintings, deriving no doubt from his old interest in architecture and the influence of Léger, is matched by a deeply felt sense of color values which in turn can presumably be ascribed to his Kapist period. Among contemporary Polish artists Potworowski was one of the most sensitive to the problems of color in painting, and his postwar work was an outgrowth of the mode of painting stemming from Kapist colorism.

MARIA JAREMA. *Rhythm IV.*   p. 135

The strivings begun by Polish avant-garde artists in the interwar period to give a new shape to art were brought to a halt by the brutal German occupation of Poland. Maria Jarema belongs to this tragic generation whose artistic development was interrupted by the war. She completed her art studies in 1936 in the sculpture class of Xawery Dunikowski, the leading

MARIA JAREMA
Stary Sambor 1908—Cracow 1958
Rhythm IV, 1958
Monotype; tempera on paper; 106 x 76 cm.
National Museum, Cracow.

20th-century Polish sculptor, at the Academy of Fine Arts in Cracow. After the war she rounded off her education in the course of visits to France and Italy. In Cracow she belonged to the Young Painters Group (1945) and the Cracow Group (1957). In addition to painting, sculpture and printmaking, she also did stage design for the Cricot II company. Number IV in her *Rhythm* series illustrates the principal concerns of her mature world. Her abstract compositions are built up from flat, interlocking shapes in which she seeks to convey an impression of movement in space, as indicated in the titles of her works, such as *Penetrations, Flight, Revolution* and the like.

TADEUSZ BRZOZOWSKI. *Stove.* *p. 136*
Brzozowski entered the Cracow Academy of Fine Arts in 1936. During the German occupation he worked with Tadeusz Kantor, an artist of about his own age who was one of the prime movers of the Cracow avant-garde, in an experimental theatre group clandestinely organized by some of the city's painters. After the war, when he divided his time between Zakopane and Cracow, he took part in the principal exhibitions of both these centers as the chief exponent of a lyrical vein of abstraction. Toward the end of the

TADEUSZ BROZOZOWSKI
Lvov 1918–
Stove, 1954
Oil on canvas; 100 x 120 cm.
National Museum, Cracow

JONASZ STERN
Kalusz, near Stanislavov 1904—
Tablet II, Red
Collage; 120 x 79.5 cm.
National Museum, Cracow.

ADAM MARCZYNSKI
Cracow 1908—
Concrete, 1960
Mixed medium, wood; 118 x 79 cm.
National Museum, Cracow.

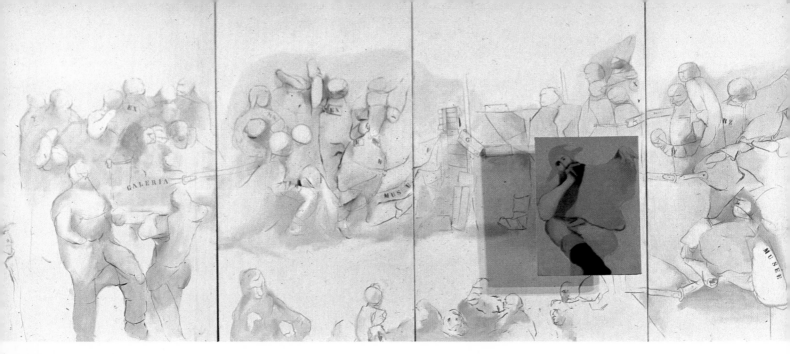

fifties he began to make frequent journeys abroad, becoming a member of, among others, the Phases Group in France as well as the old avant-garde Cracow Group which was revived in 1957. He has taught at art schools in Cracow, Poznan and Zakopane. Although painted with a great feeling for color, Brzozowski's paintings sprang from the reaction among the young postwar generation against the Post-Impressionist tradition of the Kapists. Their content tends to bring out the lyrical qualities of prosaic situations, objects and people observed with a sense of humor and of the absurd, with a

TADEUSZ KANTOR
Wielopole, near Rzeszow 1915—
Emballage, 1975
Acrylic on canvas; 250 x 500 cm.
National Museum, Cracow.

KAZIMIERZ MIKULSKI
Cracow 1918—
Nocturnal Rehearsal, 1954
Oil on canvas; 77 x 70 cm.
National Museum, Cracow.

skeptical attitude toward provincial standards and values. A striking feature is a pursuit of technical perfectionism rare in contemporary art. Beautiful effects of depth and richness of texture are produced by means of scumbling in a manner worthy of the best traditions of the old masters.

JONASZ STERN. *Tablet II (Red).* *p. 136*

Stern studied under Jarocki, Pautsch, Axentowicz and Kamocki at the Cracow Academy of Fine Arts in 1929–34. His avant-garde outlook and radical politics propelled him toward the similarly minded young artists banded together in the Cracow Group formed at the beginning of the thirties. He rejoined it when it was revived after the war and was also associated with the Young Painters Group. He is a retired professor of the Academy of Fine Arts in Cracow. His mature work of the postwar period evolved logically in the direction of abstraction. In the sixties he began to experiment with dead natural materials (bones, skeletons, fish scales), piecing them together into disturbing collages evocative of the tragic but inexorable evanescence of the world which only art can overcome. He now pastes onto his works these animal remnants from which he extracts new structural values, conjuring up a surreal world of forms which, though abstractly flat, reveal nevertheless through their projection a true third dimension.

ADAM MARCYNSKI. *Concrete.* *p. 137*

Marcynski's studies at the Cracow Academy of Fine Arts, completed in 1936, were supplemented by visits in 1930 and 1936 to France and Spain and, after the war, in 1956 and 1959, to Italy and Switzerland. He has taught at the Cracow Academy. In his avant-garde explorations he has steered a course similar to the Cracow group. In *Concrete* we have an example of the mature period of his work in which can be seen a search for esthetic values in such "manipulated" materials as rusty scraps of metal, cracked and grimy boards, and the like. From such debris, often combined with new materials, he constructs abstract relief compositions, sometimes with kinetic elements which through alterations of position produce new effects.

JERZY NOWOSIELSKI
Cracow 1923—
Woman in Darkroom, 1971
Oil on canvas; 79.5 x 120.5 cm.
National Museum, Cracow.

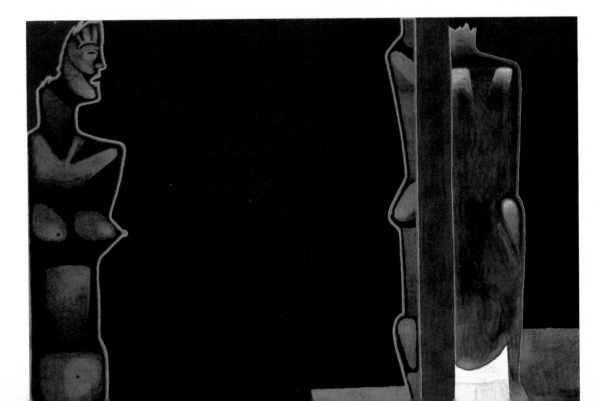

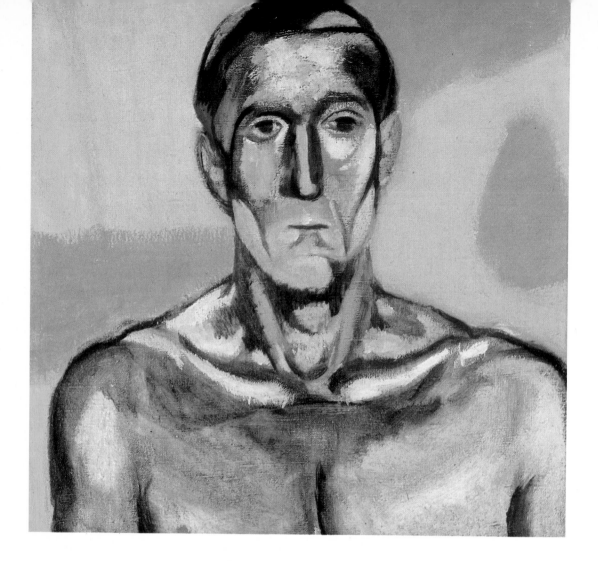

TADEUSZ KANTOR. *Emballage.*   *p. 138*
Kantor studied under Pienkowski and Karol Frycz at the Academy of Fine
Arts in Cracow in 1934–39. During the German occupation, when all artistic activities were banned, he organized clandestine exhibitions and formed
an experimental theater group from which his now world-famous Cricot II
company directly derives. His art education was rounded off after the war
during visits to Switzerland (1947) and France (1947, 1955). He belonged to
the Young Painters Group which explored new paths for Polish postwar
art. Since 1957 he has been associated with the avant-garde Cracow Group.
He is also an art theorist and theater pioneer. His work has passed through
a variety of phases: from Surrealism, practiced in the years immediately following the war, to *Informel* and, since 1965, to Happenings. He has written
two manifestoes: *Emballage* (1963) and *Multipart* (1969). In 1975 the National Museum in Cracow invited seven leading Polish artists to produce, in
conjunction with the international congress of the AICA association of art
critics that was to be held in Poland, pictures evoking in a contemporary
spirit the tradition of national art triumphant in the 19th century and so
richly represented in the Gallery of Polish 19th-Century Art in Cloth Hall
on Cracow's Market Square. Kantor's response to this commission was
Emballage, through which he confronted the ideas of Jan Matejko (1838–
93) as specifically embodied in the latter's *Prussian Homage* (1882). In it he
shows the chief figures of the Matejko vision of the might and glory of Po-

ANDRZEJ WROBLEWSKI
Vilnius 1927—killed in Tatra Mts., 1957
Rainbow Head, 1957
Oil on canvas; 62 x 62 cm.
National Museum, Cracow.

LESZEK SOBOCKI
Czestochowa 1934—
The Good Shepherd—Self-portrait of the Artist, 1978
Oil on fiberboard; 90 x 90 cm.
National Museum, Cracow

land in the 16th century stowed in packing-cases prior to removal to the lumber-room of History. The one exception, painted as a living being in the same pose as in the Matejko picture, but on a separate, projecting apron of blood-red wood, is Stanczyk, the court jester of King Sigismund I, remembered by posterity not only for his wit, but chiefly for his sage reflections on the Polish experience and the often tart words of wisdom he dared to utter in the royal presence. Kantor's equally defiant work is a contemporary statement on the historiographic legacy which asserts that only the critical mind can be a force shaping the present and the future.

KAZIMIERZ MIKULSKI. *Nocturnal Rehearsal.* *p. 139*
For many years after the war Mikulski was the art manager and resident stage designer of the "Groteska" puppet theatre in Cracow; prior to that, during the German occupation, he had been one of the Cracow painters who formed the experimental Cricot II theatre group. In 1945 he became a member of the Young Painters Group and in 1957 of the revived Cracow Group. Since 1955 his work has been related to Surrealism. In *Nocturnal Rehearsal* the surrealistic elements lifted out of their natural setting create, in a stage-like atmosphere of artificiality, new poetic values typical of Mikulski's paintings in the late fifties.

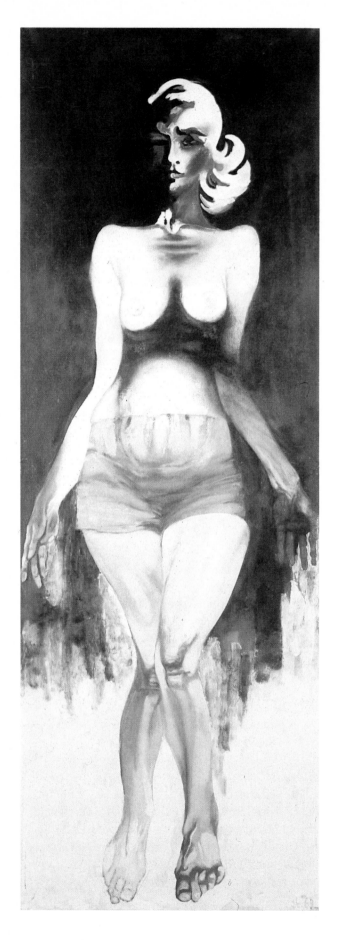

ZBYLUT GRZYWACZ
Cracow, 1939—
Stripped (Orant X), 1969
Oil on canvas; 190 x 68 cm.
National Museum, Cracow.

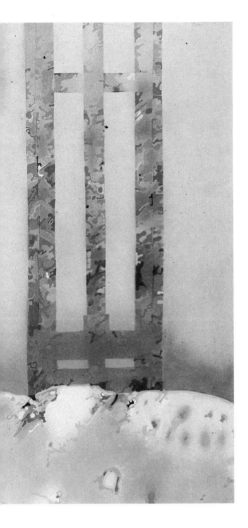

ZBYSLAW MAREK MACIEJEWSKI
Zawiercie 1946—
Spleen, 1979
Tempera, acrylic, on canvas; 137 x 200 cm.
National Museum, Cracow.

JERZY NOWOSIELSKI. *Woman in a Darkroom.* p. 139

Nowosielski graduated.from the Academy of Fine Arts in Cracow in 1947 and had been a member of the Young Painters Group since 1945. In addition to easel painting he also practices decorative art. In his youth he was fascinated by icon painting, and his distinctive picture space in slender canons of delicately outlined figures and the use of fulguration to suggest lightning, often stems from a powerful transformation of the artistic values of old icons. These transformations are so profound that his paintings verge on abstraction.

ANDRZEJ WROBLEWSKI. *Rainbow Head.* p. 140

Wroblewski's work took shape in the bleak climate of the dogmatic fifties. After taking a degree in art history at Jagiellonian University in 1948 he engaged actively in propagating the new tasks placed before art in People's Poland. At the Cracow Academy of Fine Arts, from which he graduated in 1952, he organized, in 1948, a discussion club and an autodidact group. Rebelling against the teaching methods then in favor at the Academy, he tried to develop avant-garde achievements into a new program making art comprehensible to the broader public. Pursuing this goal, he arrived at interesting results in an expressionistic, figurative mode. The people in his pictures, represented in empty spaces by means of flat areas of color, bear the marks of human solitude and alienation. His pioneering *oeuvre* has triumphantly survived his premature death in a climbing accident.

LESZEK SOBOCKI. *The Good Shepherd.* p.141

In 1966 a group called "Wprost" (Straight Out) was formed in Cracow by some young graduates of the Academy of Fine Arts (Maciej Bieniasz, Zbylut Grzywacz, Leszek Sobocki and Jacek Waltos). In 1969 they summed up their artistic credo in these terms: "To speak straight out means to express what springs from the act of experiencing in a direct, candid manner unobscured by conventions. . . . Where meaning is concerned, appearances are less important. . . . We are trying to create a state of author and spectator being co-present in the world of visualization of our experience." In the situation of Polish art at that time this reaction against estheticism and insistence on communicability had a refreshing impact. The sources of this stance can be traced back to the endeavors of Cracow artists in the immediate postwar period as exemplified by the "autodidact group" and especially Andrzej Wroblewski. An obvious influence on the Wprost philosophy was also exercised by another Cracow painter, Adam Hoffman.

Sobocki's *Good Shepherd* is one of sixteen self-portraits in which the pose, dress, expression, and even the accessories bear a close relationship to the imagination of the outstanding Symbolist, Jacek Malczewski.

ZBYLUT GRZWACZ. *Stripped (Orant X).* p. 142

Painted in 1969 by a graduate of the Cracow Academy of Fine Arts and charter member of the Wprost group who took part in all its exhibitions, this picture is a good example of his effort at that time to find an unhackneyed way of articulating his ideas about the destructive effect of stereotypes on forming judgments about human existence. The problems of developing a language capable of communicating the meaning of human feelings are a recurring theme of Grzywacz's work. Images of women

143

TADEUSZ GILLERT
Cracow Crib, 1972
Wood, cardboard, tin foil; 210 x 130 x 56 cm.
City of Cracow History Museum

trapped in art by all manner of implications are given a tragically deformed cast. In the avoidance of explictness of form can be seen not so much idle *jeux* with impulsively applied, splashing colors, as an expression of the artist's dilemma in restating a belief in the creative power of emotion.

ZBYSLAW MAREK MACIEJEWSKI. *Spleen.*   *p. 142*
Maciejewski studied at the Cracow Academy of Fine Arts under Waclaw Taranczewski and since the seventies has regularly exhibited in painting shows elsewhere in Poland. He also designs for the stage. The central theme of his work is the psychological condition of man struggling with the difficulties of life amidst the shams of a civilization, riding roughshod over accepted value systems, or eking out a lonely existence in the contemporary world. His *Spleen*, with its characteristic void of sophisticated, tonally cold color space, is arresting chiefly because of the nervously painted, acutely disturbing facial expression. In his own words, Maciejewski's object is to make "the formal and color construction of his pictures stir the deeper levels of the viewer's consciousness and subconsciousness."

TADEUSZ GILLERT. *Cracow Crib.*   *p. 144*
The Cracow crib had its antecedents in the popular Nativity play tradition and was originally part of a live dramatic entertainment. Performed by actors hailing from the populace, it comprised the following elements: portable scenery based on the architecture of Cracow, a text studded with topical and satirical allusions often accompanied by popular melodies, and puppets. The heyday of the crib as vernacular theatre came in the second half of the 19th century and was a typical feature of Christmastide customs in the poorer quarters of Cracow. Its tradition inspired the city's cabarets, notably the "Green Balloon" which flourished at the beginning of the 20th century. To revive this old tradition, the Corporation of Cracow in 1937 began to organize an annual competition for crib-makers, held in Market Square, and after the hiatus of the German occupation it has been continued to the present day by the History Museum of the City of Cracow. Though in its present form the crib is no longer a dramatic entertainment, the use of topical mottos and patriotic effigies illustrating contemporary events or anniversaries of memorable occurrences make it a kind of pageant which has replaced the spoken allusions of the past with symbols and placards serving the same purpose. The crib, usually a wooden frame on to which are pasted multicolored pieces of paper and metallically gleaming strips of foil, has a symmetrical composition and skillfully evokes the architecture of Old Cracow. Favorite motifs are the late-Gothic and Renaissance buildings: the spires of churches, especially Our Lady's, the arcades of Collegium Maius, the royal castle on Wawel Hill, the domes of chapels (more often than not the Renaissance Sigismund Chapel), the eaves of Cloth Hall, and the like. Most of them are richly lit from the inside, and the figures are moved by clockwork. The tradition of making Nativity cribs was originally connected with the families of the masons living in the Cracow suburb of Zweirzyniec, and the credit for passing on the style preserved to this day is thought to belong to one of these, Michal Ezenekier.
The cribs constructed today tend to be the joint work of people from more than one walk of life, which may include university graduates, ordinary workmen and schoolchildren. It is nevertheless a skill that remains largely a

MASTER OF THE PIETÀ
Active in Siena c. 1350–80
The Crucifixion, 3rd quarter 14th century
Tempera on wood; 37 x 24 cm.
Czartoryski Collection,
National Museum, Cracow.

male preserve and one that very frequently still runs in the family. The crib shown here won the first prize at the 1972 competition.

MASTER OF THE PIETÀ. *The Crucifixion*. p. 146

Acquired by the Czartoryski family, probably at the auction of the Toscanelli collection in 1883, this picture was originally the upper section of a polyptych. The composition is symmetrical, and the content of the scene indicates the narrative type of Crucifixion with a large number of figures, but without the Thieves. It is the work of a Sienese painter of the third quarter of the 15th century and embodies this school's distinctive lyricism. The composition is compact, and the delineation of the figures simplified and geometrical, which invests the picture, despite its small dimensions, with a truly monumental quality. The color range, restricted to flatly ap-

Facing page
GIOVANNI DA GAETA
Active in Naples and Gaeta mid-15th century
Mater Misericordiae, 1448
Tempera on wood; 215 x 137 cm.
Wawel State Art Collections, Cracow.

CUCEDE·NOS·FAMVLOS·TVOS·QS·DNE·DS·PPETVA·METIS·ET·
CORPIS·SANITATE·GAVDELE·ET·GLORIOSA·BTE·MARIA·SEP·
VIGNIS·ITECESSIONLA·PNTI·LIBERA·TRISTICIA·ET·ETERNA·
PFLVIT·LETICIA·PSPO·DOMINV·NR·

plied reds, blues, greens, yellows and whites blending into greys, is supplemented by the liberal use of gold in the ground and halos. The rich patterning of the latter engraved on the support is typical of medieval Sienese painting.

Touches of the style of Ambrogio Lorenzetti and other Sienese artists have been noted, but on balance the picture has been attributed to the Master of the Pietà, so-called from the *Pietà* in the Detroit Institute of Art.

SEBASTIANO MAINARDI
San Gimignano 1450—Florence (?) 1513
The Virgin Adoring the Child,
end of 15th century
Tempera on wood; 52 x 42 cm.
Wawel State Art Collections, Cracow.

GIOVANNI DA GAETA. *Mater Misericordiae.* p. 147

This *Mater Misericordiae,* inscribed with the date 1448, compared with mid-15th century paintings from other Italian centers clearly reveals the late-Gothic traditionalism of the artist. His lyrical style developed under the influence of Leonardo da Besozzo, a Lombard who was also active in Naples, and of Spanish painting, echoes of which are apparent in medieval Neopolitan painting. Affinities with Umbrian art have also been perceived: in the kneeling donor and the Medici arms and crowned eagle in the upper corners there is reason to believe that it was painted after a visit to central Italy. It is the earliest known dated work of a painter who was chiefly active in Naples and Gaeta around the middle of the 15th century.

SEBASTIANO MAINARDI. *The Virgin Adoring the Child.*

This painting has also been attributed to the workshop of Domenico Ghirlandaio and bears a very close resemblance to a *tondo* by David Ghirlandaio in the Strossmayer collection in Zagreb. A number of versions of this composition exist in various European and American museums. Authorship has

LORENZO LOTTO
Venice 1480—Loreto 1556
*The Virgin Adoring the Child with Saints John
the Baptist, Joseph, Francis and Catherine,*
c. 1508
Oil on wood; 40 x 29 cm.
National Museum, Cracow.

been ascribed to Mainardi, the brother-in-law, pupil and most gifted collaborator of Domenico Ghirlandaio, on the grounds of the features of style evident in the lyrical type of the face of the Madonna and the rather stiff modeling and stocky proportions of the body of the Child.

The picture was donated to the Wawel State Art Collections in 1934 by a well-known Polish collector, Leon Pininski (1857–1938), a professor of Roman law at the University of Lvov who was also active in politics.

LORENZO LOTTO. *The Virgin Adoring the Child with Saints John the Baptist, Joseph, Francis and Catherine.*

This leading Venetian painter traveled widely around Italy, absorbing the influences of Raphael, Correggio and Giovanni Bellini—particularly evident in his early work of which this Madonna and Child with Saints is an example. The painting bears the signature *L. Lotva* inscribed on the side of the stone bench and probably dates from c. 1508. The features of Lotto's work in this period are balanced composition, individualized portrayals of the figures, and solidity of drapery, as clearly manifested in this example.

LEONARDO DA VINCI.   *Portrait of a Lady with an Ermine.*
This is in all probability a portrait of Cecilia Gallerani, a lady-in-waiting at the court of Lodovico Sforza in Milan and Il Moro's mistress, although a later inscription in the upper left corner, "La Belle Ferronnière Leonard D'Awinci," alludes to a mistress of Francis I of France. The background of the picture and some of the ornamentation of the dress are later additions. That it is the work of Leonardo is strongly suggested by the style evident in such features as the pose of the sitter (more elaborate than in Italian portraiture of this period), the masterly play of light and shade on the face which bears no trace of brushwork, and the modeling of the slightly bony right hand holding the soft, white-furred animal. Zoologically, it is not clear whether the latter is a stoat in its winter coat or its domesticated albino cousin, the ferret, used in Italy for hunting. But whatever the classification, it embodies a pun, since another of Lodovico Sforza's nicknames was Ermellino ("ermine"), while the Greek word for ermine—*galée*—is an oblique reference to the name of the sitter, Gallerani.
The painting was bought, as a work by Leonardo, in Italy around 1800 (its earlier history from the 16th to the late 18th century is unknown) by Adam Jerzy Czartoryski for his mother Izabela who placed it in the picture gallery in the Gothic House at Pulawy where it remained until the November Insurrection of 1830. Because of Czartoryski's active part in this uprising, the Pulawy collection was in danger of being confiscated by the Tsarist authorities and part of it was removed to Paris (Hôtel Lambert). The collection was brought back to Poland in 1876 and housed in Cracow. During World War I the painting was stored in Dresden. Shortly before September 1939 it was taken for safekeeping to Sieniawa where it was commandeered by the Germans and hung for a while in the quarters of Governor-General Hans Frank in Wawel Castle. In 1944 it was in Frank's residence in Bavaria. After the war it was located by the Polish-American claims commission and brought back to Cracow in 1946.

LEONARDO DA VINCI
Anchiano, near Vinci 1452—Amboise 1519
Portrait of a Lady with an Ermine, c. 1485
Oil on wood; 54.4 x 39.3 cm.
Czartoryski Collection, National
Museum, Cracow.

MASTER OF THE HALF-LENGTH
FEMALE FIGURES
Active Antwerp (?) 1st half 16th century
Mary Magdalen Writing,
Oil on oak; 54 x 40 cm.
Czartoryski Collection,
National Museum, Cracow.

MASTER OF THE HALF-LENGTH FEMALE FIGURES. *Mary Magdalen Writing.*

In early 16th-century Netherlands there appeared a large group of half-length portrayals of fashionable ladies shown writing, reading or playing a musical instrument. Their activities and the objects surrounding them, painted realistically and in detail, seem to have been chosen for allegorical meanings. The subject of this particular picture has been thought to be St. Mary Magdalen as a court lady or an allegorical representation of the sense of Sight.

The physical appearance of the women in these paintings—with their typically high foreheads, lowered lids and smoothly combed hair parted in the

WORKSHOP OF DIERICK BOUTS
Haarlem c. 1420—Lowen 1475
The Annunciation, c. 1470
Oil on oak; 47.8 x 33 cm.
Czartoryski Collection,
National Museum, Cracow.

middle—has led some scholars to suppose them to be the work of various Netherlandish artists active in the second quarter of the 16th century and closely associated with humanist circles among the urban elite. Despite the lack of convincing evidence, they have been attributed, among others, to Lucas de Heere and Jan Vereycke. It cannot be ruled out, however, that these pictures, somewhat austere and monotonous in form, might have originated from various workshops.

WORKSHOP OF DIERICK BOUTS. *The Annunciation.*   *p. 153*
The monumental simplicity of a sparsely furnished interior painted with the attention to detail of a 15th-century Netherlandish realist forms the background for an intimate representation of the Annunciation. In style and

ALESSANDRO ALLORI
Florence 1535—Florence 1607
Portrait of Francesco de' Medici, before 1565
Oil on panel; 98 x 79 cm.
Wawel State Art Collections, Cracow.

JAN VAN NOORT
Amsterdam 1620—Amsterdam 1675
Portrait of a Boy, c. 1654
Oil on panel; 168.5 x 116.3 cm.
Wawel State Art Collections, Cracow.

coloring as well as composition, there are echoes of the work of Rogier van der Weyden whom the painter of the picture, if we assume that he was Dierick Bouts himself, could have met in the northern Netherlands. Other scholars believe that—produced to satisfy private religious needs—it might be the work of an artist under the influence of Bouts who certainly had followers in the Netherlands. A record of this smallish picture first appeared in 1869 in the Paris catalogue of the Czartoryski Collection.

ALESSANDRO ALLORI. *Portrait of Francesco de' Medici.* *p. 154*
This Florentine Mannerist, whose style owes much to Agnolo Bronzino, his uncle and teacher, painted the portrait of Francesco I de' Medici (1541–81), Grand Duke of Tuscany and an eminent art collector. The picture was

155

probably painted before 1565, following his return to Florence from Rome where he had become acquainted with the art of Michelangelo. The young Medici is seated in a Mannerist, unadorned interior beside a table which merges into the flat dark-brown background. The elaborately arranged hands hold a closed book and a miniature portrait of a woman who has been identified as Joan of Austria whom Francesco married in 1565. The studied elegance of the sitter's pose and the added air of distinction lent by his attire make this a good example of Mannerist court portraiture in late 16th-century Florence.

JAN VAN NOORT (?). *Portrait of a Boy.*   *p. 155*
Active in Amsterdam from 1644 to 1676, van Noort was strongly influenced by Flemish painting, particularly Jacob Jordaens. On the evidence of the inscription on the pillar at right, the *Portrait of a Boy* represents a nine-year-old young dandy, painted in 1654. His foppish attire, more in tune with the styles favored by Hispano-Flemish court circles than with the simplicity of Dutch dress, is in itself an indication not only of the sitter's social background, but also of van Noort's attachment to the court mode of Flemish portraiture.

HARMENSZ REMBRANDT VAN RIJN. *Landscape with the Good Samaritan.*
Only a few of Rembrandt's more than 600 paintings have landscape as their principal subject. The *Landscape with the Good Samaritan*, inscribed at bottom right, "Rembrandt f. 1638," came into the possession of M. D. van Everdijck, a Hague collector, in the 18th century. In 1766 it was acquired at an auction of the latter's pictures by De Cros, and in 1773–4 it featured in the catalogue of the collections of Vassal de Saint-Hubert in Paris. In 1774 it was bought by Jean-Pierre Norblin, a French painter employed by the Czartoryski family at their seat in Pulawy, and no doubt brought by him to Poland; in 1828 it was mentioned in the catalogue of the Gothic House at Pulawy, the first Polish museum, founded in 1801. Around 1831, following the November Insurrection of 1830, it came to the Hôtel Lambert in Paris as part of the Czartoryski Collection. After this had been returned to Poland in 1876, the picture reappeared in 1892 in the catalogue of the Czartoryski Collection in Cracow. The story of the Good Samaritan, drawn from the Gospel of St. Luke (Ch. X, 30–37) was a theme to which Rembrandt returned several times in the course of his life; but the Cracow picture is the only known version in the form of a painting.

The composition follows the formula of Mannerist landscape painting that became current in the Netherlands at the turn of the 16th to 17th centuries. This can be seen in the scenic treatment of the trees on the right, with a road running into the background on which are situated three figures and the Samaritan carrying the wounded wayfarer in the direction of Jericho. The left half of the picture is occupied by an open, partly sunlit view with a coach-and-four traveling toward a cluster of buildings standing at the foot of sheer cliffs that form the horizon. This unreal, stormy setting, laden with a highly dramatic atmosphere achieved by purely painterly means, is charged with symbolic meaning, stressing the element of human tragedy by setting it amid the clashing forces of nature. It is the most outstanding work by Rembrandt in Polish collections.

HARMENSZ REMBRANDT VAN RIJN
Leiden 1606—Amsterdam 1669
Landscape with the Good Samaritan, 1638
Oil on oak; 46.5 x 66 cm.
Czartoryski Collection,
National Museum, Cracow.

JOOST SUSTERMANS. *Portrait of Francesco de' Medici.*
This Flemish painter, trained by Cornelis de Vos and Frans Pourbus the Younger, made his way in 1616 via Paris to Florence where in 1620 he became court painter to Cosimo II de' Medici. He also worked for Emperor Ferdinand II in Vienna and Pope Urban VIII.

The portrait of Francesco de' Medici, who died in 1634 at the age of only twenty, was thought to be the work of van Dyck and was bought as such in Italy by the Tarnowski family. At the beginning of this century it was attributed to Sustermans by C. Hofstede de Groot. The coloring and the texture of the thickly applied paint in the light sections of the picture make it one of the best portraits painted by Sustermans, who did in fact owe much to the influence of van Dyck.

JAN LIEVENS. *Portrait of a Young Man.*   *p. 159*
Lievens was a contemporary of Rembrandt with whom he worked from 1625 to 1631 and under whose influence he remained in his early years. After studying under Pieter Lastman in Amsterdam (1619–21), he spent varying periods of time in England, Antwerp, Amsterdam and The Hague. Other influences on his work were Caravaggio and Flemish painting. The *Portrait of a Young Man*, once thought to be a self-portrait, is modeled in composition on the portrait of a youth by Raphael which was in the Czartoryski Collection in Cracow, was removed by the Germans during the last war and has never been recovered. Compared to the geometrical symmetry of the Raphael, Lievens moved the figure slightly to the right and gave him a more relaxed pose, producing a composition of great vigor in the Baroque spirit. It has been painted in the cosmopolitan manner of Baroque court portraiture in which Flemish elements played their part. Its form bears a close relationship to the portraits of van Dyck. Although there is no signature, Lievens' authorship is firmly indicated by the landscape background which resembles that of an autograph portrait of a young woman, dated 1650, which was once at the Walker Art Center in Minneapolis.

TOURNAI WORKSHOP. *Legend of the Swan Knight,* detail.   *p. 160*
Around 1879 Stanislaw Gorski donated to the Augustinian monastery in Cracow a tapestry depicting a Burgundian version of the Swan Knight legend. It had been damaged in a fire in 1863, and the monks cut off and sold the part which had suffered most; it is now in the Osterreichisches Museum für angewandte Kunst in Vienna. It is thought that two similar tapestries were destroyed during the fire on the Gorski estate. Family tradition has it that all three had been brought to Poland from France or Spain by Stanislaw Gorski's father, who had been a general in the Napoleonic army. In 1921 the Cracow tapestry was presented to the Wawel museum as a longterm loan. It and the other two doubtless originally formed a set which was part of the decoration of an apartment.

The surviving tapestry contains seven scenes from an early 13th-century *chanson de geste* whose subject was Godfrey of Bouillon, the leader of the First Crusade, and his family. Some of the scenes have a commentary in the North Picard dialect.

It has been established that the tapestry was bought in 1462 from Pasquier Gremier—the biggest producer and seller of tapestries in Tournai—by Philip the Good, Duke of Burgundy, for Cardinal Jean Jouffroy, Bishop of Ar-

JOOST SUSTERMANS
Antwerp 1597—Florence 1681
Portrait of Francesco de' Medici, c. 1633
Oil on canvas; 113 x 84 cm.
National Museum, Cracow.

JAN LIEVENS
Leiden 1607—Amsterdam 1674
Portrait of a Young Man, c. 1660
Oil on canvas; 100.5 x 81 cm.
Wawel State Art Collections, Cracow.

ras. Nothing is known of its history after the death of the cardinal until its arrival in Poland. The cartoon is thought to be the work of an artist associated with Robert Campin and Rogier van der Weyden. The rich, though not over-ornate composition, the concern for realistic depiction of detail evident in the drapery of the clothes, the meticulous drawing of jewelry, and the courtly elegance of the pose of the figures make the Wawel tapestry an outstanding example of Burgundian court art in the late Middle Ages. Notable also is the almost portraitlike representation of the features of contemporary personages, such as Charles the Bold, Philip the Good and Isabella of Portugal, among the legendary figures. The sophistication and air of melancholy apparent in the facial expressions of the actors in this story convey the autumnal quality of an era drawing to a close in the life of a medieval court.

TOURNAI WORKSHOP
3rd quarter 15th century
LEGEND OF THE SWAN KNIGHT, 1460, detail.
Wool tapestry, with silk and gold threads; 413 x 479 cm.
Wawel State Art Collections, Cracow.

HISTORY OF THE COLLECTIONS
IN THE MUSEUMS OF CRACOW

Founded in 1879, the National Museum possesses one of the richest and certainly the most comprehensive collection (650,000 objects) of Polish works of art and culture from the Middle Ages to the present day, and a considerable amount of similar material from other countries. There is also a library of manuscripts, old books and records which are fundamental resources for the history of Poland and many aspects of the political and cultural history of Europe.

Polish painting and sculpture constitute the major holdings of the museum and cover all the main developments in Polish art. A gallery of prints, drawings and watercolors is one of the largest in Polish museums. European painting is represented by works from Italy from the 13th to the 18th centuries (the most valuable being Leonardo da Vinci's *Portrait of a Lady with an Ermine*), the Netherlands (notably Rembrandt's *Landscape with the Good Samaritan*) and France (16th to 18th centuries). The collections of handicrafts and national memorabilia, textiles and costumes, arms and coins, are not only of great antiquarian interest but also include objects of unique curiosity and esthetic importance. Noteworthy also by the standards of this part of Europe is a Far Eastern department with very valuable collections of Chinese porcelains and Japanese woodcuts, in addition to objects from India, Indochina, Korea, Mongolia and Tibet. A small, but good archaeological section contains Mesopotamian, Egyptian, Greek, Etruscan and Roman antiquities. Finally, there is the largest Polish collection of Byzantine art in the country, consisting of icons primarily from the Carpathian area, but also from the Balkans and Russia.

The National Museum's holdings are housed in a number of separate buildings—most of them historic structures located in the center of Cracow, comprising the following departments:

Gallery of Polish Art to 1764, building of the Szolayski Foundation. Opened in 1928, the gallery also houses arms and armor, Orthodox art and Far Eastern art for study purposes. On display is a rich collection of medieval sculpture, painting (including the Kruzlowa *Virgin and Child*) and stained glass acquired from churches and monasteries, chiefly in Cracow and southern Poland; also modern portraits, history pieces and religious paintings by native or locally active artists.

Gallery of 19th-Century Polish Art, on display in Cloth Hall since 1883. Famous history paintings by Jan Matejko, and canvases (also a few sculptures) by outstanding Polish artists, e.g., Piotr Michalowski, Henryk Siemiradzki, Aleksander Gierymski, Jacek Malczewski and Jozef Chelmonski.

Gallery of 20th-Century Polish Art, New Building, opened in 1950. The premises are now being enlarged to form the main building of the Museum. The display of contemporary painting and sculpture includes works by Tadeusz Makowski, Olga Boznanska, Stanislav Wyspianski, Jozef Mehoffer, Wojciech Weiss, Tadeusz Kantor and many younger artists. There are also collections of applied arts and handicrafts available for study purposes, and a library and reading room.

Czartoryski Collection. Founded in Pulawy in 1801, subsequently transferred to Cracow, and since 1950 a section of the National Museum. Permanent display of historical records, handicrafts, arms and armor and a gallery of European painting (Lorenzo Lotto, Leonardo da Vinci, Rembrandt). Collections of prints and antique art available for study purposes.

Emeryk Hutten-Czapski Collection. Czapski Palace, founded 1903. Coins, prints, drawings and watercolors, also rare books and manuscripts available for study purposes and exhibited for alternating periods in the library.

Jan Matejko House, opened in 1904 in the building in which the great Polish history painter was born, lived and died. A biographical museum, it displays the original interiors, memorabilia, Matejko's art collection and many of his paintings and sketches.

164

Czartoryski Library, housed since 1961 in a new building with a collection of rare books and records open to scholars.

WAWEL STATE ART COLLECTIONS

Founded in 1920, the collections comprise five permanent displays: *Royal Apartments*, with a unique set of tapestries and carefully chosen paintings, sculptures, furniture and art objects (e.g., porcelain and clocks) which form harmonious but stylistically varied interiors corresponding to their original use and appointments. Among the paintings of particular interest are the portraits of rulers and prominent figures in the political and intellectual life of the old Commonwealth and history paintings commemorating important political events and victorious battles. There is also a rich display of European paintings, especially Italian, Dutch and Flemish, which were brought to Poland in considerable quantities.

Crown Treasury, with what has been rescued and recovered (from the looting by the Prussians during the occupation of Cracow in 1794–6) of royal insignia, historical memorabilia—including arms and armor, insignia of orders, emblems of military and state office, gifts received by kings, banners—goldsmith's work and objects made of other costly materials.

Oriental and Middle Eastern Collections. The tastes of Polish kings and nobles, and in due course much of the landed gentry, led to the purchase of items of costume modeled on Eastern fashions. In particular, Wawel accumulated the gifts presented by Persian, Turkish, and Tatar envoys; and to these were added the trophies brought back from the expedition to Vienna by King John Sobieski in 1863. Especially noteworthy among the rich collections so assembled are a set of Turkish tents and their furnishings, tapestries, banners, caparisons, saddles and arms.

Ancient Wawel constitutes the findings of research into the earliest history of Wawel arranged on the site of the remnants of the oldest excavated buildings. As throughout the Wawel Museum display and unique architectural setting merge together.

ETHNOGRAPHY MUSEUM

Founded in 1910 and the property of the city of Cracow, The Ethnography Museum contains the most comprehensive and oldest collection of objects relating to Polish folk culture, plus similar material brought by Polish antiquarians from nearby European countries: the Ukraine, Byelorussia, Germany, Austria, Bohemia, Moravia, Slovakia, Russia and Lithuania. There is also a more fragmentary display of objects of ethnographical interest from various parts of Africa, the Middle East, South America, Asia and Oceania.

JAGIELLONIAN UNIVERSITY MUSEUM

The University Museum was formed in the 18th century when the objects which had accumulated along with the library of the University were
turned into a separate *Camera Raritatis*, comprising numerous and very

varied curiosities linked with Polish culture and learning in general through the history of the University and grouped under the heads of history, art and scientific instruments (which had been collected since the 15th century, chiefly in the field of astronomy). These collections of the memorabilia of distinguished scholars, artists, statesmen and university patrons, furniture, gems, coins, medals and plaster casts are displayed in the partly preserved and partly restored interiors of the Collegium Maius, a university building erected in the 15th and 16th centuries. This gives the University Museum a quality exceptional among such institutions in Europe.

HISTORY MUSEUM OF THE CITY OF CRACOW

The collections of this municipal museum founded in 1945 illustrate the history and culture of the city in all its varied forms and so are not all of a kind. The basic material consists of iconographical objects, townscapes and portraits, local handicrafts and memorabilia. Among the last, the Silver Cockerel of the still surviving Brotherhood of Bowyers (1565) and the insignia of the town council (1532) stand out.

The main permanent display, in Krzysztofory Palace on Market Square, presents the history and culture of the city. Important sections housed in separate premises, one devoted to the history of theater in Cracow, another—the Judaic Museum—to the history and culture of the city's Jewish community. The latter is in the Old Synagogue, the oldest preserved building of this type in Poland (late 14th century). There is also a small exhibition of town council records in the tower which is all that survives of the old Town Hall.

SELECTED BIBLIOGRAPHY

BANACH, J., ed. *Krakow miasto muzeow* (Cracow, City of Museums). Warsaw, 1976.

BIALOSTOCKI, J. *The Art of the Renaissance in Eastern Europe—Hungary, Bohemia, Poland.* Cornell University Press, Ithaca, New York, 1956.

BIALOSTOCKI, J. M. WALICKI. *Malarstwo europejskie w zbiorach polskie* (European Painting in Polish Collections). Warsaw, 1955.

DABROWSKI, J., ed. *Krakow, jego dzieje i sztuka* (Cracow, Its History and Art). Warsaw, 1956.

DOBROWOLSKI, T. *Nowoczesne malarstwo polskie,* I–III (Modern Polish Painting, I–III). Wrocklaw-Warsaw-Cracow, 1957–64.

DOBROWOLSKI, T., DUTKIEWICZ, J., ed. *Wit Stwosz, Oltarz krakowskie* (Wit Stwosz: the Cracow Altarpiece). Warsaw, 1964.

DOBROWOLSKI, T., ed. *Historia sztuki polskiej, I–III* (A History of Polish Art, I–III). Cracow, 1965.

JUSZCZAK, W., LICZBINSKA, M. *Malarstwo polskie,* (Polish Painting: Modernism). Warsaw, 1977.

Katalog zabytkow sztuki w Polsce, IV. Miasto Krakow (Catalogue of Art Treasures in Poland, IV: the City of Cracow). Part I, Wawel, ed. by J. Szablowski, Warsaw, 1965. Parts II, III, ed. by A. Bochnak and J. Samek, Warsaw, 1971, 1978.

KOZAKIEWICZ, S. *Malarstwo polskie, oswiecenie, klasycyzm, romantyzm* (Polish Painting: Enlightenment, Classicism, Romanticism). Warsaw, 1976.

LEPSZY, L. Cracow: *The Royal Capital of Ancient Poland: Its History and Antiquities.* New York, 1912.

RHODES, A.: *Art Treasures of Eastern Europe.* London, 1972.

ROSTWOROWSKI, M., ed. *The National Museum in Cracow. II: The Czartoryski Collection.* Warsaw, 1978.

SZABLOWSKI, J., ed. *Zbiory zamku krolewskiego na Wawelu* (The Collections of the Royal Castle on Wawel). Warsaw, 1975.

SZABLOWSKI, J., ed. *The Flemish Tapestries in the Royal Castle on Wawel.* Warsaw-Antwerp, 1975.

WALICKI, M. *Malarstwo polskie, gotyk, renensans, wczesny manieryzm* (Polish Painting: Gothic, Renaissance, Early Mannerism). Warsaw, 1961.

WALICKI, M., TOMKIEWICZ, W., RYSZKIEWICZ, A. *Malarstwo polskie, manieryzm, barok* (Polish Painting: Mannerism, Baroque). Warsaw, 1971.

WALICKI, M., ed. *Sztuka polska przedromanska i romanska do schylku XIII w.* (Polish Pre-Romanesque and Romanesque Art to the Close of the 13th Century). Warsaw, 1971.

Photograph credits

S. Jablonska: Frontispiece
K. Jablonski: p. 38
Z. Kamykowski: pp. 71, 72, 83, 89, 95, 136 (top), 138 (top), 140
A. Kedracki: p. 100
S. Markowski: pp. 33, 43, 58, 64, 65, 67, 91, 92, 94
S. Michta: pp. 26, 44, 51, 54, 78, 125, 147
J. Myszkowski: pp. 24, 25, 101, 110, 111, 112, 114, 116, 129, 130, 138, 149
K. Pollesch: pp. 20, 60–61, 62, 82, 87, 96, 118, 119, 120, 121, 124, 126 (top), 126 (bottom), 127, 128, 131, 132, 133, 134, 146, 152, 153, 158, 159
B. Rogalinski: pp. 18, 23, 28, 29, 32, 36, 45, 50, 53, 73, 80, 81, 104, 108, 109, 135, 144, 148, 151, 155, 157, 160
J. Romero: p. 117
L. Schuster: pp. 22, 34, 35, 49, 68–69, 74, 75, 76–77, 79, 85, 97, 98, 102–103, 154
W. Smolak: pp. 31, 47, 48, 55, 56 (right), 56 (left), 57 (right), 57 (left), 63 (top), 63 (bottom), 99, 113, 114 (bottom), 115, 122, 123, 136, 137, 139, 141, 142 (left), 142–143
A. Wierzba: 59, 88, 106
L. Schuster and A. Wierzba: pp. 39, 40–41, 42, 84
CAF, Warsaw: p.21

INDEX OF ILLUSTRATIONS

INDEX OF NAMES

The numbers in italics refer to names cited in the captions

GENERAL INDEX